# the Singles Tax

# the
# Singles Tax

NO-NONSENSE
FINANCIAL ADVICE
FOR SOLO EARNERS

## Renée Sylvestre-Williams

ECW

Published by ECW Press
665 Gerrard Street East
Toronto, Ontario, Canada M4M 1Y2
416-694-3348 / info@ecwpress.com

Editor for the Press: Jen Knoch
Copy editor: Crissy Boylan
Cover design: Caroline Suzuki

LIBRARY AND ARCHIVES CANADA CATALOGUING
IN PUBLICATION

Title: The singles tax : no-nonsense financial advice for solo earners / Renée Sylvestre-Williams.

Names: Sylvestre-Williams, Renée, author.

Description: Includes bibliographical references and index.

Identifiers: Canadiana (print) 20250284294 | Canadiana (ebook) 20250284308

ISBN 978-1-77041-823-3 (softcover)
ISBN 978-1-77852-527-8 (ePub)
ISBN 978-1-77852-528-5 (PDF)

Subjects: LCSH: Single people—Finance, Personal.

Classification: LCC HG179 .S95 2026 | DDC 332.0240086/52—dc23

This book is funded in part by the Government of Canada. *Ce livre est financé en partie par le gouvernement du Canada.* We also acknowledge the support of the Government of Ontario through the Ontario Book Publishing Tax Credit, and through Ontario Creates.

Canada   Ontario 🌼   ◎ ONTARIO CREATES

PRINTED AND BOUND IN CANADA          PRINTING: MARQUIS    5  4  3  2  1

To my parents, my brother, sister-in-law and friends.
You've always encouraged me to (finally) write a book.
Thank you all for the support.
Mom, it's not quite the book we talked about,
but we're finally here.

# Contents

# Hi, I'm Single and I Worry About Money

In 2016, two sisters, Betty Wilsack and Margaret Renouf, based in Caribou Island, Nova Scotia, had had enough. They had lived together in Betty's house for 38 years, splitting all the bills, and Betty helped to raise her sister's son. Despite sharing what some might call an economic household or unit — a group of two or more people who live in the same house and are related to each other by blood, marriage, common-law relationship, adoption or foster relationship — the sisters weren't entitled to the survivor's pension from each other's government pensions. They'd lived together for most of their lives, raised a child together and shared the economic burden of the home, but because they didn't share a bed, they had fewer rights and benefits than a couple.

The women wrote to their local member of parliament and to the minister of Families, Children and Social Development, but almost a decade later, people still have to be married or in a sexually active common-law relationship to get survivor benefits.

Betty and Margaret might not be the type of person you think of when you think of single people, but they're part of an ever-growing club. Single people are everywhere, and they don't all live like the characters in *Sex and the City*. Maybe they've never been partnered, or maybe they're divorced or widowed. They might have kids, or they might proudly be childless cat ladies. They're the bartender in Miami, Florida, who complained about subsisting on unhealthy Uber Eats food rather than wasting groceries or buying smaller quantities at a premium. They're the African YouTubers living abroad who can't afford the high price of being single *and* sending money back home.

They're me. I grew up immersed in the propaganda of coupledom: the happily ever after, the "I dreamtof my wedding since age five" stereotype, the ultimate adulting badge that is getting married and having children. Single people were and are portrayed as sad cats left out in the rain, thank you, J.D. Vance. If you remember, the senatorial hopeful said in 2021 that the U.S. was being run by Democrats, corporate oligarchs and "a bunch of childless cat ladies who are miserable at their own lives and the choices that they've made and so they want to make the rest of the country miserable too." This man clearly never owned or was owned by a cat.

But most of us single people aren't sad. We're not automatically drowning in loneliness or sitting around waiting for our life to begin. We have rich relationships; they just may not involve sex and sharing the bills. Studies show that single people, specifically women and childless women, are among the happiest subgroup of the population, according to an article in the *Guardian* that referenced Paul Dolan, a professor of behavioral science in the Department of Psychological and Behavioural Science at the London School of Economics and Political Science. Unfortunately, the stigma of being single can make some single women feel unhappy, given society's emphasis on marriage and children.

There are also a lot of us. Data from the last census done by Statistics Canada found that in 2021, 4.4 million Canadians lived alone. That's 15 percent of all adults aged 15 and older in private households, the highest proportion on record. (In 1941, solo dwellers were only 6 percent.) When you put those numbers in the context of housing, just under three in ten households contain only one person. Those numbers don't include single parents living with their children or single people living with a roommate (which was the fastest-growing household type). A 2025 documentary from Jatinder Dhillon found that Canada has one of the highest rates of solo agers (single people, usually over 50) in the world.

Yet Canadians aren't alone in the living alone. In the U.S., just under three in ten people live alone (28.5 percent) and, in countries like Germany, Norway and Finland, the number goes up to 40 percent. A 2023 government survey in Japan found single-person households were the most common living arrangement, making up 34 percent of all households.

Despite these huge numbers, when I started writing about personal finance, I noticed the industry was almost unfailingly focused on people who were, or expected to be, partnered up. I used to pitch articles about singles finances, and a lot of them were turned down. Yet this wasn't a niche audience. Where was the financial information for us?

I got tired of wondering when traditional financial education was going to focus on solo earners. So in 2020, I got annoyed enough to start my own newsletter, *The Budgette*, which focuses on solo earners, and this book extends that work. I figure if I've got questions on *all* things money, you do too.

Questions like: Can I afford to retire? Can I afford to turn down a gig with terrible pay? Is it possible for me to own a home? Do I need a will? Does it have to cost more when I travel alone? Can I afford to be a single parent without waiting for a partner? Can I make sure I'm cared for when I'm in my golden years? In fact, can I live like a Golden Girl? (I'm definitely Dorothy.)

I'm right there with you, tapping numbers into a calculator and pondering the state of my retirement funds. I know I'm not alone in wishing there was some kind of guidebook on how to be single *without* the goal of being partnered. When singles finances are talked about in the media, it's usually simplistic recommendations about housing (get a roommate!) or buying food in bulk (where would I put it?). It's never about the long-term financial disadvantage of not being able to create a recognized economic unit with your best friend like you can with a spouse.

Why didn't someone tell me that I should have a team of people to advise me on things like contracts, investments and retirement? Why didn't someone tell me that I should consider disability and critical illness insurance when I decided to go freelance? Why don't people talk more about co-op or co-living options? In fact, why aren't there more co-op or co-living options? Why did I have to find out about outlining my estate plan from doing this for a living? *The Singles Tax* is here to provide the context, advice and reassurance that I wish I'd had.

Here you'll get a solo perspective on saving for retirement, spending, housing, traveling, taxes, wills and estates, and insurance. From the tax code to hotel rooms, we'll look at the policies that exclude or punish single people. Then we'll look at what's happening to change those policies, what we can do personally (that's the personal part of personal finance) and what needs to be done on a political level.

While the definition of the family unit has evolved over the years to include queer and unmarried couples, single people have been left out of the progress parade. As finance writer Ellen Roseman said to me, "In Canada, our income tax and pension systems no longer discriminate against couples who cohabitate without getting married. But singles can't take advantage of tax-saving vehicles such as pension income splitting in retirement." You better believe we're going to be discussing why that's the case.

Even when it comes to day-to-day expenses, the singles tax is a real thing. The Royal Bank of Canada found that singles pay 66 percent more in rent compared to couples and 27 percent more in "household operations," such as phone, internet and housekeeping.

Let's look at a sampling of expenses from the period between 2019 and 2021 in Canada (though the same patterns hold true elsewhere).

| Per year | Single | Single parent (with two children) | Couple (with two children) |
| --- | --- | --- | --- |
| After-tax income | $32,200 | $56,100 | $103,900 |
| Rent | $21,468 | $21,468 | $21,468 |
| Food costs | $3,391 to $3,780 | $8,742 | $14,767 |

You might say that the couple spends more due to higher rent for a bigger space and higher food costs, but they also have more advantages when it comes to shared costs and tax advantages. So, in short, single people spend more on the essentials of life and have fewer systemic privileges that can help them build and share wealth.

No wonder single people tend to feel more anxiety about money. We're doing it alone. We're making the money, we're the key investors, and we support any dependents on one salary. If we lose our job, there isn't a partner's salary to fall back on. Plus, if we grew up in a culture that frowned on talking about money, we're not even sharing our concerns with friends or learning about money from them. Too many of us are shouldering that financial burden alone. No wonder more than 40 percent of Canadians, 77 percent of Americans and 33 percent of people in the UK cite money worries as one of their top reasons for stress.

Just like any other stressor, financial worry can take a massive toll on your mental and physical health, quality of life and your relationships. But the key to curbing that gnawing anxiety? Getting your financial life in some kind of order. I'm in your corner, and I'll show you how to build a team; being single doesn't mean you have to deal with this alone.

Ready to push back against the singles tax? Let's go.

## CHAPTER 1

# Building a Team (Because You Need One)

When you're single, you do most of the work. You're the primary wage earner, cook/chef, cleaner, accountant, coach, etc., as I told my dad when he eyed some dust on my television set. I don't know about you, but I find that's a lot to carry and sometimes I just want to lie down on my couch and sleep forever. That's why delegating to a team can help. If you can afford it, pay the experts (or at least some financial and administrative software) to do the work for you. Instead of spending hours doing your taxes, you can use that time to do something else — yes, this includes lying on your couch.

Most of us don't work with experts unless we have to; we think we have to be rich to work with an accountant, adviser or planner. It's hard not to think that when you're told you don't have enough investable assets (that's the liquid stuff — your brokerage and retirement accounts and trusts) to make it worthwhile for someone to take you on as a client. But many professionals work on a fee-for-hire basis, which means you don't have to be the Monopoly man to use their services. These experts may also save you money in the long run, so consider it less an expense and more an investment.

If you're undergoing a change in marital status (either becoming single or coupling up), these experts can be extra important in protecting your best interests through the transition.

With that in mind, who should you have on your team?

## ACCOUNTANT OR BOOKKEEPER

If you have a fairly complicated tax situation or just don't want to do your taxes, a good accountant or bookkeeper is definitely well worth the cost, which you can claim as an expense if you're an independent contractor or business owner. A bookkeeper does things like monthly bank reconciliations and financial statements, payroll processing if that's part of your business and year-end financial and tax documents for your accountant. An accountant reviews and analyzes financial statements, files tax returns, gives tax advice and does tax planning for you so you can meet your goals.

An accountant can also help you if you have a growing business and you need to figure out payroll and manage all the taxes, rent and other expenses. This leaves you free to focus on more exciting things like hiring, research and development and business development.

Plus, they can give you great advice. One of the best pieces of advice I ever got was from my former accountant. I had just bought my home, and he said that if I ever coupled up, I should have the other person sign a cohabitation agreement. I had no idea that in Ontario, a cohabitation agreement outlines the rights and obligations of each partner during and after a relationship. Check your province, territory or state for something similar.

There is also software that can help you out — accounting apps like FreshBooks, Wave and QuickBooks can track your invoices, mileage and time worked — but a human can make sure you're using your online tools effectively.

Now, a bad accountant can get you in hot water with the tax man if they do something like forget to file your taxes. Check their references thoroughly. You also do not have to stick with the same accountant for your entire life. It's perfectly fine to use one during a complicated tax year or if you're new to filing taxes and switch to tax software once you've got a handle on things. There are options out there for all incomes like TurboTax, TaxSlayer, H&R Block and UFile.

Tax software ranges from free to pay what you can and all the way up to a few hundred dollars for TurboTax's full-service self-employed tier. If you want an accountant to take care of your income tax filing, that could range from $150 to $1,000 depending on how complicated your situation is.

What about using AI to help with your taxes? That's a tough one. If your taxes are simple, you probably won't need to use AI. If your situation is more complicated, and you ask AI questions about certain tax deductions, I would still double check with an expert as AI can give you incorrect answers. So, consider hiring that accountant.

## LAWYERS

Though no one wants to engage a lawyer before they have to, I think people should know or have the names of the following types of lawyers. You might be thinking that you could get references when you need them, but consider a scenario where you have been laid off or a family member has died. You're under stress and you're worried about paying bills or making funeral arrangements. Will looking for a lawyer be your top priority in that moment? Plus, we tend not to make the best decisions under stress.

## Wills and estates lawyer

You can absolutely create a will on a platform like Willful in Canada or FreeWill in the U.S., if it's a simple one. (More on that in the chapter on wills and estates.) If you have a complicated will that involves trusts or a business, then working with a lawyer can help you articulate your desires before and after you die.

Another reason to know a lawyer who specializes in wills and estates is that at some time in your life, you may become an executor of a family member's or friend's will and need some advice. I know two people who are working their way through this process, and it has been fairly complicated.

If you do talk to a lawyer about your will and estate, here are some questions you can ask them:

- How often should I update my will or estate plan?
- What happens if I own property in multiple provinces, states or countries?
- How can I protect my estate from potential legal disputes or challenges?
- How should I choose an executor, and what responsibilities will they have? (You can also talk about payment for them because being an executor is a job and often a thankless one.)
- What happens to my digital assets (e.g., online accounts, cryptocurrencies, NFTs) after I pass away?
- How can I ensure my minor children are looked after if something happens to me?
- What steps can I take to avoid probate or make the process easier for my heirs?
- What documents do I need to create a comprehensive estate plan?
- How can I minimize estate taxes for my beneficiaries?

## Employment lawyer

If you get laid off, you'll benefit immensely from clear legal advice from someone who is not affiliated with your former company. An employment lawyer can review your severance package and advise if you are entitled to reasonable notice and compensation based on your contract and severance package. Believe me, some companies will offer you the barest minimum, like one company who laid off a group of us, offered me one week severance because I'd been there less than a year, and offered one more week with an air of "See how nice we are?"

I took my severance package to an employment lawyer, referred to me by a friend and instead of two weeks, I got 12. As a solo earner who might be out of work for a while, it's especially important not to leave money on the table and to know what rights you have, such as your employer can't pressure you to agree to a severance package until you've talked to a lawyer.

I have also asked employment lawyers to review contract offers for specific wording to ensure I could continue doing projects outside business hours without fear of the company attempting to claim ownership of them or getting fired for a conflict of interest.

Here are other questions you can ask an employment lawyer:

- Can my employer fire me without cause? What are my rights if they do?
- Do I get severance pay and how much?
- Is my noncompete agreement enforceable? (Places like Kansas and Nebraska don't have statues governing noncompetes and usually let the courts figure it out.)
- What should I do if I'm experiencing workplace harassment or discrimination? (This is really important these days with companies rolling back DEI initiatives.)

- Can my employer change my job duties or reduce my salary without my consent?
- What are my rights if I need to take medical, parental or bereavement leave?
- How do I negotiate an employment contract or severance package?
- What should I do if my employer is retaliating against me for speaking up about workplace issues?
- Do I have a case for wrongful termination?

## Family lawyer

A good family lawyer can reduce the amount of grief you experience during a divorce or separation. Even if you're on great terms with your soon-to-be-ex, you're going to be newly single, and you want to ensure you're on solid ground. Each situation is different, but here are some general questions to ask a family lawyer:

- What are my rights and obligations during separation or divorce?
- How are child custody and visitation determined, and what factors influence the court's decision?
- How is child support calculated, and can it be modified later?
- What is spousal support (alimony), how is the amount determined and how long does it last?
- How are marital assets and debts divided in a divorce?
- What should I include in a prenuptial or postnuptial agreement?
- How do I protect my assets in case of separation or divorce?
- What are my options for resolving family disputes outside of court? (e.g., mediation, where the couple hires

a neutral third party who helps them negotiate a balanced agreement, or collaborative law, where a lawyer advocates for you)

## FINANCIAL ADVISER OR PLANNER

While the finance bros of Reddit are dying to give you some free advice, do yourself a favor and pay for it instead.

A qualified adviser can help you assess your current financial situation and help you figure out your short-term (taking a vacation, paying off student loans or renovations), medium-term (buying a home, starting a business or having kids) and long-term goals (retirement planning or divesting your business).

They can also provide advice on the right financial products for your specific needs and review and update your plan, goals and investments as needed. Keep in mind that some financial advisers (including ones at major banks) receive a commission for selling you certain funds or products, and others are paid a percentage of your assets. If you want unbiased advice, seek out a fee-based or fiduciary adviser with no sales agenda. Look for someone who is a certified financial planner (CFP) so you know they have the skills to do the job and that they're expected to adhere to a code of ethics.

An adviser can do more than run the numbers: They can provide calm advice when the market gets dramatic and you feel the urge to sell everything and stuff the money under your mattress, and they can advise on whether you should invest in that totally sketchy, sounds-like-a-pyramid-scheme company.

Some questions to ask an adviser:

- How many years of experience do they have?
- How do their fees work?

- What sort of clients have they worked with? Can they provide references?
- What's their minimum asset requirement? (This is for advisers who get paid a percentage of your assets' worth to manage them.)
- What's their investment philosophy?
- How long do their clients stay with them?
- How do they measure success?
- Who will handle my portfolio?
- What does asset protection mean to them?
- Do they have experience in areas like tax optimization, philanthropy and business?
- How do they stay current on trends?
- What platform and tools do they use? How secure are those tools?
- How do they communicate with clients, and how often?
- Can I call them whenever I have a question?

Don't hesitate to ask questions. If they make you feel uncomfortable, don't work with them. It's your money and future, not theirs.

If you're going through a major breakup, don't skip this step. One planner, who asked to be anonymous when we spoke, said that if it's an amicable separation, it might be easier to have the separation conversation with the help of a neutral third party or mediator. They can help you figure out what you're trying to accomplish. "Are they looking to get advice on debt? Are they looking to get advice on assets? Are they looking to get advice on cash flow? When I have a conversation with clients like that, I would ask what they're trying to accomplish and then tailor my questions."

You may have questions about building or rebuilding credit scores, especially if finances were blended. In that situation, talk to your bank and credit card companies, because your financial picture depends in part on whether you were the lead on the mortgage, credit card and property assets. If there's property involved, the planner said that it's also important to have the conversation about what's going to happen to the family home. "Are you going to sell it? Are you going to rent it? Is your partner going to buy it out from you? Are they going to pay you fair market share for it? That's where speaking to a financial planner and going through that together can help."

The planner had one last piece of advice: create an emergency fund (which we'll talk about more in chapter 3). That fund can help you pay for time with a lawyer, a financial planner or for your first and last month's rent.

## INSURANCE AGENT OR BROKER

Why an insurance agent or broker? Aren't they trying to sell you something? Yes, but a good insurance agent creates an insurance plan that suits your needs and should, ultimately, help you feel more secure. They can advise on life insurance, home and auto insurance, business insurance and critical illness and disability insurance. Since they work for a specific company, they provide you with policy options from the company they represent. If you want to shop around a bit more, work with a broker. They work for the customer and can sell you a policy from multiple insurance companies. You are their client.

Your agent or broker should be able to answer your questions, explain your policy and even help you make a claim. However, be sure to shop around to make sure you're getting the best deal. Loyalty doesn't get you a lower rate on your home insurance, as I found out. My home insurance had constantly ticked up so when I finally sat down and shopped for comparables, I saved about

$20 a month for the same coverage. Not bad. (Of course, that $20 got spent somewhere else, probably on my cellphone bill since I live in Canada.) Comparing insurance policies is easy. Sites like Ratehub in Canada and Progressive in the U.S. ask you to enter your information and give you a quote in minutes.

Now, working with an agent or broker isn't a one-and-done situation. You should check in with them at least once a year to make sure you've got enough coverage for your current situation. If things change — say you start making more money or you have children — definitely talk to them.

## HOW DO YOU FIND THESE PEOPLE?

Start with recommendations from your friends and family. Ask them who they like and why they like them. Listen to their answers: Do they like their accountant because they can hand over a box of receipts and T4 slips or their Excel file to them and just have to sign the tax documents? Do they like the attention to detail?

If you're looking for an accountant, talk to your friends, family and coworkers who are in similar tax situations as you and get the name of their tax preparer. Some may specialize in corporate or cross-border taxes, for example. You don't want to be stuck at tax time scrambling to find someone who knows how to deal with the IRS as well as the CRA.

Once you have a list of names, double check that they're licensed in your state or province by checking their working and licensing associations. For example, you can check the law societies of the state or province to see if there have been any complaints against a lawyer.

Next, interview them. Ask them all the questions and *do not feel embarrassed* about what you don't know. That's why you're talking to them. If you get a bad feeling or just don't vibe with them, trust your instincts. I don't care if your closest friend or your parents really like them, if you don't, why would you trust your money or tax preparation to them? (This is why so many women leave their adviser within a year after the death of their spouse or partner.) Remember: These are going to be long-term relationships so make sure that you're comfortable with each other.

Most experts won't charge a fee for a quick informational call, but make sure you ask them before you set up an appointment. When I was considering incorporating my business, I spoke with two accountants for about 30 minutes each. I had my questions ready and made use of the set time.

## YOUR FRIENDS

Your friends, with their various backgrounds and experience, can be hugely helpful in money matters. If you ask my closest friends, they'll tell you that we discuss money *all the time*. We talk about salaries, negotiation tactics and whether a restaurant might be too expensive. I discuss freelance fees with other writers when asked. I'm a big fan of talking about money because it helps us negotiate better salaries, rates, phone plans, vacations, cars, mortgages, etc. Knowledge is power.

Speaking generally (because all cultures and families are different), the average person is shy about discussing money and finances with family and friends for fear of being judged.

I reached out to Susy Fossati, the director of Avignon Etiquette, to ask, "Why is talking about money still a big taboo, and how do we change that?" She explained, "It starts with British etiquette, which is very much Canadian. It's an indirect culture. We'll ask someone 10 or 20 questions around the topic.

It's the same with finance. We'll beat around the bush tactfully trying to get to the answer, but that will always be the way versus just asking."

She admitted that it's a battle she often faces because of her Italian background, which is a very direct culture, but having been raised here, she also has a lot of that indirectness. "I get both sides, and you have to respect both sides." Coming from a fairly direct culture myself, I've had to learn how to be indirect out of the fear of offending people. (Which is very tiring and annoying.) But how can you respectfully discuss money without having to ask 10 to 20 questions?

There's no one answer, Fossati said. It's about gauging each person's comfort level. The more you know someone, the more you know where their sensitivities lie. "And again, it's all about being respectful of their boundaries and how much they're willing or unwilling to share." I'd also add that it helps to lead with vulnerability and transparency. Let people know you're not just being nosy; you're looking to learn, share information and grow. When a publisher asked me for my rate to write them an article, I asked several writer friends what I should charge. One of them told me what she made. I asked for that and got it. Thank you, Karen.

Americans are a little more direct than Canadians, but they're also not that great talking about money. A 2023 survey by Wells Fargo found that 82 percent want to keep money a private topic — especially when it comes to their savings and earnings. Speaking of earnings, according to America's National Relations Labor Board (NRLB) you have the right to communicate with your coworkers about your wages, and you can also talk about them to labor organizations, worker centers, the media and the public. (I am writing this in 2025, so hopefully the NRLB still exists and hasn't been completely DOGE-ified.)

On the plus side, the taboo about talking about money seems to be fading among younger people, which is amazing. Let's help each other save or make more money.

## THE TAKEAWAYS

- Make a list of experts before you need them. Ask your friends for recommendations.
- Check experts' credentials with the relevant society or association.
- Ask them questions. They're either going to be managing your money or advising you, so you want to be comfortable with them.
- Ask about fees and how they work. Keep asking until you understand.
- Talk about money with the goal of learning and growing. Be willing to share your knowledge.

## CHAPTER 2

# Housing
# (Why Four Walls and a
# Roof Are So Expensive)

There's a running joke in one of my friend circles that if we ever pooled our resources and lived together, we'd need a cat room. We daydream about what our space would be like beyond feline accommodations: Everyone would have their own bedroom with en suite bathroom, naturally. We'd have a communal kitchen and living space, so we could hang out and get some friend time in. We'd have a housekeeper come in once a week, and as we get older, maybe a nurse to check in on us. It's a great dream, and I think we're half serious about living together, especially because half of us still rent. As my friend Diane once said, "As soon as I think I've saved enough for a down payment, prices jump."

Housing is undeniably one of the major questions of our time. In Canada, not only is homeownership out of reach for many people, but even paying rent is getting harder. A 2024 Abacus survey showed nearly three in five Canadians are somewhat or very concerned about losing their home or rental because of financial issues. And that precarity is even more pronounced for single people.

In this chapter, we'll talk about how we got here, housing options that don't require 105 percent of your income and ways we can plan for housing that supports us as we age.

## WHAT IS AFFORDABILITY?

The old rule of thumb was that housing should be 30 percent of your net income. At 40 percent, the Organisation for Economic Co-operation and Development (OECD) considers a household overburdened. Overburdened is starting to look like the new normal.

In 2025, when I wrote this, surveys found that some Canadians were spending way more than 30 percent of their income on a place to live. The median gross income for single people was $45,069, and 30 percent of that is $13,521, or $1,125 per month. The average rent for a one-bedroom apartment in Canada in January 2025 was $2,109, almost double the 30 percent guideline for a median income Canadian. The average monthly mortgage payment in 2024, according to the Canadian Mortgage and Housing Corporation (CMHC), ranged between $1,337 in New Brunswick and $2,836 in British Columbia. In the U.S., the average monthly mortgage payment in 2024 was US$2,209. California has the highest monthly payments at $2,500 compared to West Virginia's $960 (all in U.S. dollars).

But where did this 30 percent guideline even come from? I asked Dr. Carolyn Whitzman, a housing and social policy consultant who has worked as an expert adviser to the University of British Columbia's Housing Assessment Resource Tools project, which developed standardized best practices for analyzing housing needs using detailed, open data. When we spoke, she worked as a senior housing researcher at University of Toronto's School of Cities, researching best practices to scale affordable missing-middle, modular and replicable housing.

"It's both arbitrary and standard," she said. The standard part of the housing costs calculator was set by the OECD in the 1980s, and Canada has used it since. Other countries, such as the U.S., the UK and Australia, also follow this guideline.

"Back in the early days of labor rights, there was a notion of eight hours for rest, eight hours for work and eight hours for what you will. Out of that same era, there was advocacy for one day's work for one week's rent, which means 20 percent, not 30 percent. And when Canada started doing housing policy — for instance, there's a report called the Curtis Report on postwar reconstruction that came out in 1944 — they used 20 percent as their standard of affordability, which slowly crept up to first 25 percent and then 30 percent. Quebec still uses 25 percent as its definition of affordability."

The Curtis Report was produced by a committee set up to analyze and manage possible problems of postwar reconstruction, policies and programs. It used income category measures, a clear definition of affordability based on proportion of household income, as well as a housing-need assessment method that included both "accumulated needs" and future "needs arising from population growth and [affordable housing] replacement." It recommended one-third of new construction be nonprofit public housing, one-third regulated rental and one-third private market homeownership.

That sounds great, right? But the federal government decided to instead let the market decide. They put policies in place that would increase homeownership rates but ignored low-income households.

Dr. Whitzman pointed out that we're still operating under cultural assumptions that have been in place for decades. One of those ideas is that owning a home is a pathway to creating wealth. "What started happening is that our finance ministers were really worried about pensions and people living longer," she said. "So, they thought, 'Wouldn't it be great if their home was their pension fund? What if everyone, except for these failures, owned a home and when they sold the home they made a profit?'" She points out that life expectancy used to be shorter, and these days, people are living well into their eighties. In fact, if you're in your seventies, you have a 25 percent chance of living into your nineties, according to actuaries.

We're not keeping up with demographic trends in other ways either. Dr. Whitzman said that a lot of our housing policy is still locked in "the identification of a normal family that's going to do certain things and die at certain times and not get divorced. And it's just so absurd." She points out that demographics are completely different now, and those housing policies are still locked in assumptions from another century when people were expected to get married and have children in their twenties.

Something similar was happening in the United States postwar as well. Just like in Canada, the idea of homeownership as a path to creating wealth has been around since the end of the Second World War.

After the Great Depression, which began in 1929, Americans needed help to build and buy homes. The Federal Housing Administration (FHA) was established by the National Housing Act of 1934 to regulate interest rates and mortgage terms after the banking crisis of the 1930s. The federal government began to insure mortgages issued by qualified lenders through the FHA, providing mortgage lenders protection from default: If a borrower failed to make their payments, the FHA was required to cover the unpaid balance. This ecosystem meant more funding to build and buy homes and some stability in the housing market. It also cemented segregation with a process called redlining, which denied people access to credit based on where they lived. In the U.S., that disproportionately affected African Americans and other racialized groups, preventing them access to homeownership and the intergenerational wealth it can confer.

## SO WHY DID HOUSING BECOME SO EXPENSIVE?

Both income and home prices have trended upward over the last several decades, but one has rapidly outpaced the other and there is no need to guess which one. Home prices have skyrocketed in the last two decades in North America, the UK, Australia and pretty much anywhere. It really feels like the last affordable time was just before the 2008 financial crisis. In fact, the CMHC said that the last time housing was affordable compared to income was in 2004, meaning we didn't need a massive income to afford a home. The rule used to be that you could borrow up to four times your salary for a mortgage, and that was enough: The median family income in Canada in 2000 was $50,800, and the average value of a home was $163,951. In 2020, the median family income went up to $96,220, and the average house price hit $571,000. There have been fluctuations since then, but house prices have generally trended upward and overall wages haven't caught up with housing prices and the housing bubble hasn't burst.

The same happened in the U.S. The Harvard Joint Center for Housing Studies found that, in 2022, the median sale price for a single-family home was 5.6 times the median household income. That's the highest it's been since the 1970s. It also found that across the country, home prices grew by 43 percent between 2019 and 2022, while incomes grew by 7 percent during the same period. It's a little hard to afford a home when your income doesn't increase at the same rate as house prices.

In 2024, the Canadian government changed the mortgage rules, letting people take on a longer mortgage (up to 30 years) and raising the cap on mortgage insurance so people can buy a home with a down payment of less than 20 percent. This means more people can qualify to buy a home, but lower mortgage payments over a longer term mean more interest, and these homeowners might still have mortgage debt as they near retirement.

The changes to mortgage rules didn't address the fundamental problem: A shortage of housing means available dwellings fetch a higher price.

In 2023, the CMHC estimated that to restore housing affordability, the country would need 3.5 million more units by 2030. The *more* in that sentence is doing a lot of heavy lifting. It assumes 18.6 million total housing units would be available by 2030, which was revised down to 18.2 million due to material and labor costs. Other costs have also increased generally, such as financing costs, government fees, development charges, taxes and interest on money borrowed. That means development projects die. Just outside my window, I can see a large hole in the ground and there are days I don't see any construction activity. The U.S. is also short about four million to seven million homes, according to a survey done for the Pew Charitable Trusts.

Of course, these numbers just focus on *available* housing, not *affordable* housing. Even the CMHC admits that building more houses won't magically solve housing challenges for low-income people. That's because developers exist to make a profit. That's their goal, and quite frankly, we should not be expecting them to build affordable housing just because there's a demand for it. As much as I loathe to admit it, that's not their job.

It used to be the Canadian government's job. The Mulroney government put a stop to building housing in the 1992 budget, terminating the federal cooperative housing program after building nearly 60,000 homes for low- and moderate-income Canadians. Then just over a year later, in the April 1993 budget, the government froze spending for social housing, thinking that the private sector was more efficient (read: cheaper and faster) at building housing. The CMHC moved from building houses to insuring mortgages in 1999. These mortgage securitization programs provided more choice and access to mortgage financing for buyers, which meant more people had more access to mortgages, and that fueled demand and speculation, turning housing into an asset for capital accumulation. Combine that with the federal subsidies for homeowners and longstanding bias against renting, and you create a housing shortage with ridiculous prices.

Older Canadians are also hanging on to their homes longer. There was an expectation that baby boomers would downsize, freeing up homes. That hasn't happened because many boomers want to age in place. They saw what happened in long-term-care (LTC) and retirement homes during the pandemic and don't want to live there. Who can blame them? I mean, the Ontario government decided it could move people to LTCs from hospitals without their consent, and when people refused, the government fined them. Ruth Poupard, who was 83 in 2024, was fined thousands of dollars.

It's only fairly recently that the Canadian government has gotten back into building housing through the Public Lands for Homes Plan. The federal government partnered with all other levels of government, homebuilders and providers to build homes faster on underused and surplus public lands. Depending on where you look, the federal or provincial governments own the majority of land within Canada. Some estimates put it at close to 90 percent in total, with the federal government holding about 40 percent. The goal is to build 250,000 new homes by 2031. Additionally, the 2024 budget had $500 million cash for the new Public Lands Acquisition Fund. The plan was to buy land from other levels of government to use for housing for the middle class; 20 percent of those units must be affordable. Even then, that's not enough homes to keep pace with the number of people who want to buy.

In America, it's a similar story: The U.S. federal government got out of home building in 1973, when President Nixon stopped the program's funding. That has contributed to a shortage of 7.1 million affordable homes.

## AFFORDABLE HOUSING IN VIENNA

Governments *can* build affordable housing. You only have to look at Vienna, where there is not only a lot of affordable housing, but there's no stigma attached to it. A quick search reveals that in Austria's capital city, renters in affordable housing pay a third of the price compared to London, Paris or Dublin.

The City of Vienna is the landlord of about 220,000 apartments and is one of the largest government landlords in Europe. When you add in the 200,000 cooperatives (more on these shortly) that were built with municipal subsidies, more than half of Vienna's population lives in some form of affordable government housing.

How did Vienna do it? It started with a massive building program at the end of the First World War. When the Habsburg Empire collapsed in 1918, people came to Vienna, many of whom were poor and had to live in cramped, poorly lit and unventilated spaces. The City of Vienna estimates that nearly 170,000 people were living in these conditions. The crowding contributed to the spread of tuberculosis, known at the time as "the Viennese disease."

To fund a building project to alleviate these conditions, the Social Democratic Workers' Party of Austria levied a tax on the top 20 percent of rents and on luxury goods like champagne and on horse-riding. This tax, known as the Breitner tax, was introduced in 1923, and the city council decided to build 25,000 housing units. There's a great poster on the City of Vienna's website of a rich couple looking shocked as a red arm reaches into their champagne bucket to grab one of the three bottles chilling. By 1934, the City had built 65,000 units.

Then, unlike other cities, they kept building affordable housing and haven't stopped. Employees and employers now each pay a 0.5 percent income tax for social housing construction, renovation and for direct assistance to low-income residents. Because roughly 80 percent of the population qualifies for social housing, people of mixed incomes live in these units, avoiding the all-too-common stigma about subsidized housing in North America. Plus, these projects are not stuck in some remote, undesirable neighborhood barely reached by public transit. They're fully integrated in the city. Each project must be approved by a jury of experts, and the criteria isn't based on which one is the cheapest. Instead, they're chosen based on economic, socially sustainable, ecological and architectural criteria. It beats the dreary building in North America and screaming NIMBYs who are afraid of social housing tanking their home's equity.

"Due to developers' competitions, subsidized housing offers a high quality of life, taking into account factors such as communal spaces, a large share of green spaces, etc.," said Veronika Iwanowski, who works in international relations at the City of Vienna.

"This dates back to the very beginnings of our system, when the first municipal complexes were designed by renowned architects with the aim of not only offering functional but also beautiful architecture, as well as green spaces, communal spaces, doctors' practices, libraries, kindergartens, etc."

The City also supports apartments built and managed by non-profit or limited-profit housing developers with subsidies such as 1 percent interest loans for up to 40 years, which cover roughly 35 percent of construction costs. That means rents can be lower, and the City can still ensure buildings meet their criteria. Plus, since so much of the housing has lower rents, it keeps private sector rents low as well.

Do I have to add that there hasn't been an uptick in crime with social housing? I feel like I shouldn't, but every meeting I've attended as a member of my residents' association has that one person who brings up how social housing will bring "undesirables" into the neighborhood. That could be poor people, BIPOC people, immigrants or all of the above. So maybe the problem isn't them, NIMBY.

## CAN A SINGLE PERSON AFFORD TO BUY OR RENT SOLO?

I was very, very lucky when I bought my condo. It was early 2009, right after the 2008 financial crisis started and just before prices in Toronto started climbing. I took out $12,500 from my retirement account through the Home Buyers' Plan, which was less than the 20 percent needed for a down payment. I was making about $76,000 a year as a senior lifestyle editor and qualified for a $250,000 mortgage. (Those were the days.) What helped me afford my place through years of layoffs and freelance work was the purchase price and nearly 17 years of ridiculously low interest rates. It was good timing that had very little to do with financial planning on my end.

Recently I was doing my monthly troll through real estate websites, looking at condos, and I came to the realization that *I am priced out of my own neighborhood.* If I sold my place, I could afford a *smaller, less well-built* condo if I wanted to stay where I am. Or I could move out of the city, get a roommate or move to a less-expensive province. I could move back in with my parents or move in with my brother and sister-in-law. I love my family, but none of those options are appealing right now, or ever.

And just because I own doesn't mean I'm secure. I live in an area designated for high-density housing, all those 50-story condos. Rumors abound that developers have had their eyes on my building for a while so there is a lingering wait-and-see hope that an eventual offer would be sweet enough to convince the majority of homeowners in my building to sell. I imagine being close to retirement (lol) when we'd get an offer that's too good to refuse and I have to find housing right at the time when I would rather not.

I'm one of the few people in my friend group of Gen Xers and elder millennials who owns, as I mentioned at the beginning of this chapter, and I had a bit of help from my family. The rest of us rent. None of us want anything big. A little bit of outdoor space would be nice, as we all learned during the pandemic that being able to literally touch grass is good for mental health. Not worrying about whether your landlord will raise your rent (beyond the yearly increase) or renovict you is *great* for mental health.

Partners with dual incomes likely split their housing costs, whether mortgage payments or monthly rent, but we singles pay for that on our own, along with everything from utilities to condo maintenance, insurance and repair costs. For single Canadians, homeownership has become increasingly out of reach. In 2024, you needed a household income of $137,000 to buy a condo in Toronto and $195,420 to buy a single-family detached home. In Vancouver, you'd need an income of $214,460 to afford an average-priced home there. The average income in Canada is $57,100, so you can do the math.

Even for renters, carrying housing costs solo is difficult. The average rent in Canada in 2024 was $2,185, and in the big cities like Toronto, Vancouver, Burnaby and Mississauga, rents were higher. Smaller cities had lower rents, but salaries were also generally lower, and they also saw more people moving in looking for cheaper rents, which increased those rents.

This is why it's vital to maintain strong rent control — which generally limits the frequency and extent of rent increases. Rent control exists in some form in all Canadian provinces and territories, though in the U.S., 37 states outright prohibit it. If there aren't limits on landlords, tenants — especially single tenants — are even more vulnerable, and prices are primed to climb even more quickly.

Jo Pavlov, an education worker from Hamilton, Ontario, rents a two-bedroom place and said that housing costs are one of the biggest expenses of being single. They told me a few years ago, "I started [renting my current house] with a friend, and we split the bills down the middle. When she left, all responsibilities fell to me, and it's more than I can afford." Pavlov estimated that paying for all housing costs alone, including bills, ate up over 60 percent of their net income. Since speaking to Pavlov, they have found another roommate and got a raise, but they still don't think they can carry the rental cost of their apartment for an extended period.

Some people are fine with getting a roommate, but what if you're not? Maybe you are 50, 60, 65 or 70, and you want your own space to do your own thing. Maybe you have kids, so you already have roommates, and don't want another random adult around. Needing a roommate should not be the default for owning or renting. "I mean, it is an option. I think most of us have had roommates during our college years," said financial journalist David Aston. "You know, being able to live independently on one's own without a roommate is certainly something most people would aspire to because roommates are complicated. Usually people get to a certain stage of life and they like their independence."

There is no easy financial answer. One option, Aston said, admitting it was a pat answer and easier said than done, is to move to a lower-rent locale when you retire or earlier, as we saw during the pandemic when people moved out of major cities to smaller ones because the cost of housing was cheaper and they were able to work remotely.

"It's just fine being in Toronto with its high rents, and they don't want to move to Orillia or Hamilton, or somewhere beyond where the rents are a little bit lower," he said. "But it does work for some." He pointed out that many people who don't mind moving to a smaller town usually grew up in one or still have family there. They are happy going back to where they have roots and the rent is lower, but that's not the case for everyone. Moving out of your area can mean losing your network of friends, especially if no one has a car. In a smaller city, you might need a car or encounter accessibility issues if you have physical disabilities that limit your ability to walk or drive. Plus, you may not have easy access to medical help, and generally speaking, rural areas can be less progressive (according to Pew Research Center) so that's a harder sell for racialized people and those who are LGBTQ2 and want community.

Clearly, more creative options are required.

## HOUSING CO-OPS

Co-ops are back in the spotlight lately, and they might just be the secret sauce for affordable housing. Even the Canadian government is getting back into the game by increasing funding for co-ops. For single people, in particular, co-ops offer some serious financial perks that are worth exploring.

## What exactly is a co-op?

Co-op housing isn't like renting from a traditional landlord. In a co-op, the people who live in the building are also the ones who run it. When you buy into one, you become a shareholder in the co-op corporation and get the exclusive use of one unit in the property.

That means you get a say in how things operate — everything from maintenance decisions to rent increases. It's a model based on community, collaboration and, most importantly, affordability. Co-ops don't exist to make a profit, which is a huge advantage for residents because the rental rate isn't tied to market rates. Instead, rents are just enough to cover the building's operating costs, like maintenance and utilities. You have a say about increases at the annual general meeting where co-op members review the co-op's finances and budget recommendations created by the board of directors. What's really cool is that people who live in co-ops often range in age and other demographics. Plus, there are some cooperatives that focus on seniors, families or creatives.

Co-ops are not a new concept — New York City got its first in 1876, and the first north of the border was founded in 1913 as student housing in Guelph, Ontario. Co-ops really took off in the 1960s and 1970s in Canada when government lobbying resulted in funding to build more of them. For nearly 20 years, the federal government helped finance thousands of housing co-ops until, yes, 1992 when it canceled the last of the program. Ontario canceled its co-op program in 1995, and B.C. followed in 2001. Quebec is the only province to still sponsor co-ops, which is part of the reason why housing is cheaper there than in other provinces.

But let's talk about the history of co-ops.

Cooperatives exist in many sectors beyond housing, including retail, manufacturing and banking. According to the International Cooperative Alliance (ICA), which has been around since 1895, more than 12 percent of humanity is involved in one of the 3 million cooperative enterprises worldwide. While data on housing co-ops specifically is limited, the ICA reports that the largest 300 cooperatives collectively generate US$2.4 trillion in revenue and provide jobs or work opportunities to 280 million people — about 10 percent of the world's employed population.

Cooperative Housing International estimates that in the U.S. in 2018, there were 6,400 housing cooperatives with 1.2 million dwellings, which amounts to about 1 percent of the housing stock. You can find your local co-ops in the U.S. through the National Association of Housing Cooperatives.

In Canada, as of 2024 the Co-operative Housing Federation of Canada (CHFC) estimates there are 92,000 housing co-ops across the country, housing over 250,000 people. Of those co-ops, 2,200 are nonprofit. That may not sound like a lot in the grand scheme of things, but in cities like Toronto, Vancouver and Montreal, co-ops are providing affordable housing to people who might otherwise be priced out of the market. While co-ops are available in most provinces, Ontario, British Columbia and Quebec have the largest numbers. The growing affordability crisis is pushing the co-op model back into the spotlight as a real solution to skyrocketing rents and housing costs.

Various levels of government are funding the building and longevity of new co-ops. The Ontario provincial government got in on the spending in 2024. It provided co-ops with $649,790 for technical and financial advice so they can be managed and sustained for the long term. The federal government announced a $1.5-billion Canada Rental Protection Fund in the 2022 budget, which gives co-ops and nonprofits money to buy rental buildings to protect renters and to build more co-ops by 2028. It's the largest investment in co-op housing since, say it with me, 1992. (It also committed another $976 million over 2024 to 2029 to build additional affordable housing.) At the time of writing, not much progress has been made, so we'll see if they hit the 2028 goal.

## Financial advantages of co-op living for single people

Now, let's get into why co-ops make sense for single individuals. If you're living alone, without the cushion of a second income, every dollar counts. Private market rent prices, especially in major Canadian cities, are out of control. The CHFC found that the cost difference between renting a co-op and market rentals could be as wide as $500 a month. Plus, co-op rent is more stable. In the private rental market, landlords can hike up the rent whenever they want (within governmental guidelines, of course); in a co-op, the residents make those decisions.

When you move into a co-op in Canada, you usually don't need to fork over the hefty first-and-last-month rent deposits that landlords typically demand. Instead, co-ops charge a one-time membership or share purchase fee, which is often much lower than traditional rental deposits. The bonus? You often get that money back when you move out, provided the unit is in good shape and your account is in good standing. Just think — you could keep that $4,000 to $6,000 and put it toward groceries, savings, furniture, travel, an emergency fund or even a really nice dinner.

Now, when it comes to buying into a co-op, the process is different from qualifying for and getting a mortgage. You buy shares in a co-op, and if you don't have all the cash required, you can take out a share loan. It's similar to a mortgage but can be harder to get from traditional lenders because if you default, it's more difficult for them to foreclose. If you're looking for a share loan, credit unions (aka co-op banks) are your best bet.

Here's another perk: Many co-ops offer subsidized housing for low-income individuals. If you qualify, your rent would be a percentage of your income, usually around 30 percent. That's a big deal, especially if you're working part-time, freelancing or going back to school. It takes off a lot of financial pressure and allows you to allocate your money elsewhere — whether it's saving for the future or enjoying life a little more.

You can also avoid the seemingly inevitable rent increase that comes from being bounced between units: Once you're in, you're in, providing you meet your membership obligations. For single people, who are often competing with couples or people with roommates who have more income or security in the rental market, co-ops offer a reprieve. You don't have to constantly be on the lookout for the next apartment or fear being priced out of your neighborhood.

A quick note: Since they don't keep up with market pricing, co-ops don't have the same long-term opportunities for building wealth. So, be aware of that before you buy and focus on building wealth elsewhere (such as in an investment portfolio).

### Shared costs and responsibilities

Living in a co-op means shared responsibilities, and this can save you money. Members are typically expected to pitch in, whether that's helping with maintenance decisions, organizing community events or participating in building upkeep. While that might sound like a lot of work, it's actually a way to keep costs down and, yes, foster a sense of pride in your community. For example, instead of paying high fees for building management or contractors, members work together to handle minor repairs or make cost-effective decisions. As a single person, you won't be bearing the brunt of expensive management fees or dealing with individual or corporate landlords trying to push unnecessary renovations to increase rents.

Co-ops aren't just about financial savings. They're about community. This is where things like sharing resources and mutual support come into play. Whether it's swapping furniture, carpooling or even sharing meals, the sense of community can lead to indirect financial benefits. For single individuals, this can be huge. You're not on your own even though you live alone. You could have neighbors who can help with everything from lending you a tool to offering career advice or babysitting. While these might not seem like direct financial perks, they can add up in the long run by cutting down on expenses. You have the options.

## The catch, because there always is one (or two)

Okay, so co-ops sound great, right? But there are a few things to keep in mind. First, because co-ops are so affordable, demand is high. Waitlists can be long, especially in big cities. It can take years to get into certain co-ops, so if you're thinking this might be an option for you, it's worth getting on a list as early as possible. Also, co-op living requires participation. You'll need to attend meetings, vote on decisions and possibly even volunteer in some capacity. For some people, this level of involvement might not be ideal, but for others, it's part of the charm. It's about being part of a community rather than just being another renter. Decide how much interaction you want to have with your neighbors.

For single people, co-op housing offers a real financial advantage. With lower rents, stable costs and a community-driven approach, co-ops provide an alternative to the increasingly unaffordable private rental market. While there are challenges, like long waitlists and the need for participation, the benefits — both financial and social — make co-op living an option worth considering. If you're navigating the housing market alone, co-ops might just be the affordable, stable solution you've been looking for, if you're willing to wait. 2028 isn't that far away. Hold your politicians responsible.

## CO-OWNING A HOME

My friend Celia and I rented a good-sized apartment in Toronto's Davisville neighborhood for nearly five years. It was about 900 square feet, which was perfect for two tall women and a cat. The apartment had two bedrooms: One was a whole square foot bigger than the other, so Celia got that and her cat got the extra square foot . . . and the rest of the apartment, including the bathroom and my bedroom, sometimes.

The apartment was right on the subway line, everything except cable and phone was included and we paid, wait for it, $1,100 when we moved in together and $1,400 when we moved out. Total. That included utilities.

When we decided to look for condos to buy, we originally talked about pooling our mortgage approvals and finding a two-bedroom place for us and future cats. We found an agent and started looking. (The cat stayed home.) We wanted to stay in the city as we both worked in it and didn't own cars. And there *were* two-bedroom condos, but the rooms weren't the same size. One would be the average size of a condo bedroom (10 x 12 feet) while the other would be a den, which, no, real estate agents — if it doesn't have a door, it's not a room. I don't care what your fisheye-lens photographs say. It's a large nook.

Eventually, we became dissatisfied with what we were seeing. We talked and realized that while we were friends, there were small things that irritated us about each other. Celia didn't like the fact I delayed doing dishes until I absolutely had to (I still do this, which is why a dishwasher was on my must-have list), and I wasn't a huge fan of cat hair everywhere. Cats, yes. Cat hair, not so much. I shed enough. So, we ended up buying our own places and we're still friends.

We may not have become co-owners, but other people are making it work. In Toronto, six people ranging from their late twenties to late thirties made headlines by pooling their money to buy a $1.3-million house together downtown. There were no couples or family members among the six. Just friends. They named the house Clarens Commons and secured a co-ownership mortgage, which may have been the first in the country from a big bank.

I spoke with Valery Navarrete, one of the original owners and residents of Clarens Commons about how they made it work. Prior to Clarens Commons, she had lived alone and with a partner, and now her goal was to live in a stable community rather than buy a house as a financial investment. "We're very much coming from the housing-as-a-human-right kind of perspective," she said. "We were just seeing friend after friend find a place, be happy to stay for a while and then get renovicted."

While the goal was to create a community, Navarrete said they did their due diligence around finances. "When you're co-owners and you're all on the lease, you are all individually responsible if suddenly your other co-owners don't meet their commitment. So we did look into that, but primarily for us, we were looking for the experience of living in community, which is one of really intermingling our lives together and relying on each other and having fun together."

The co-owners not only hammered out the tangible financial responsibilities, but they also talked about the intangibles. They created a spreadsheet where they each individually filled in their fiscal information and then talked together about it. "We dubbed it financial nudity," she said. "It was equal parts 'What's your income and what are your expenditures?' and 'How did your family treat money? How did you grow up? What are your current views on money? Have they changed?'" She said that they did later have conversations about a renovation, budgets and how people felt about the idea of borrowing more money.

While it was difficult to find an institution that had a formal mortgage offering for more than four people on it, Navarrete said that's changing: "Since then, we've realized that with a lot of banks, if you have a relationship, and you go and talk to them, they can make it happen."

They ran into the same issue when looking for home insurance, and again, it was relationships that helped them get insurance. They had to pay a slightly higher premium than a couple likely would have, but they were satisfied securing insurance so they could get the mortgage. Still, this kind of trailblazing wasn't all angst and stress. "There were some really humorous moments as well," she said. "We were with the lawyers who handled the transfer, and we were filling out forms, and there wasn't enough room for all of our names."

Navarrete moved out due to a change in her personal life circumstances, but she would absolutely do it again. She said that once her child is an adult, she and her partner would move back into a house like Clarens Commons. "In those five years of living on my own, I think I had done quite a good job of it. I had a lot of friendships; I had a busy work, volunteer and social life. I could fill what would have been solo time with hangouts with friends, and I felt really full in terms of my sense of community and connection. But it was a lot of work to just coordinate all of that. I would have a Sunday to myself, and I would go do my groceries and get organized for the week ahead and cook some food, and I would go, 'Oh, you know what? It would be really nice to eat with someone, but who's around?' That was my desire, with co-owning and co-living, to have more built-in connection."

The co-living option is a popular one. Phil Levin founded a co-living compound in Oakland, California. When he experienced the impact of community on well-being firsthand, he launched Live Near Friends, which helps you find locations in the U.S. where you can build co-living spaces. "Every group of people that lives together should have some sort of community agreement. It should be short and simple and be based on principles rather than rules," he said in an email. "It doesn't need to be a formal legal document, and people should anticipate that it will be a living document. If it doesn't fit on a notecard, it's too long! This covers the 'What are the principles of our community?' bits."

However, if the agreement involves owning property together (which not all communal living arrangements do), Levin said you need a more formal legal document (drafted by a real lawyer) describing the rules about usage, decision-making and exit from the entity. This might be an LLC agreement (if you own as a limited liability company), a TIC agreement (if you own as a tenancy-in-common) or a condo association.

If you are renting to friends and you are the owner, you should have a lease agreement. If you are a master tenant and you are subleasing to friends, you should have a sublease agreement.

While not all single people are lonely (there's a big difference between solitude and loneliness), social isolation and loneliness are recognized by the World Health Organization as a priority public health problem and policy issue across all age groups, and thoughtful co-living could be one way to help address that. The joy of this kind of arrangement is that you can seek companionship when you want and retreat to your own space when you need to relax and recharge.

## DOING IT ON YOUR OWN — CONVERSION

When there's a gap, things rush in to fill it. Water, air, weeds, people. When there's a gap in housing, people try to fill it. One option is to create your own development corporation if you're willing to take on a whole new build, from the ground up, or modifying a home to suit your current needs.

Now, before I continue, I have to tell you it is not affordable at all, by the metrics set by the CMHC. It takes a lot of planning and a lot of money.

A few years ago, I spoke with Martha Casson, who has always had an interest in shared housing. She said that the Ontario government in her estimation has not provided enough funding for municipalities to provide the infrastructure for different types of housing. "A builder friend of mine wanted to build a shared ownership home, and we've been talking about that and he put in for a building permit," she said. "I was not to be a resident of that, but it was turned down [in 2017] by our municipality."

"The whole idea of people living together to lessen the burden of costs was a no-brainer," John, the builder, said. He had experience with shared housing, having lived in a farmhouse along with his grandparents, aunts and uncles.

Casson told me that the councillors of their municipality had never dealt with "such an animal before," and Casson and her friend weren't sure the councillors understood what they were trying to do. They made five deputations to the council to create a zoning order; this was around the same time of a comprehensive zoning order change that granted municipalities in Ontario the right to do a big review of their zoning. The council kept delaying and delaying even though Casson and her friend kept deputizing. Casson said that out of the seven councillors, two were on their side, but their proposal got voted down.

The thing was, there was a lot of interest in the idea of building or retrofitting a home into apartments that could be owned individually by unrelated people. "There were parents of adult children with disabilities who'd never been in care, and the families thought, 'If we three families could buy a house together and our three adult disabled children who are working and whatnot could live with a caregiver, wouldn't that be great?' Like, there are all kinds of options," Casson said. She had a connection with the Ontario Human Rights Commission, sent some of the documentation to them and asked if this was right. But by now two years had passed, and her friend lost his deposits from the interested buyers, so he had to change his whole plan for that property.

Finally on the last deputation day, the Ontario Human Rights Commission sent a letter to the mayor *and* posted it on the website, highlighting that the zoning bylaw would impact the living possibilities of people who are protected by the Human Rights Code. Casson said after that, council came to an agreement and removed every reference to prohibiting what they had been labeling communal dwellings.

"So, wait, it took what sounds like a public shaming and pointing out a human rights violation to get this request approved?" I asked her, somehow not surprised. (Honestly, is this what housing advocates feel like all the time? I'm on my residents' association, and I am no longer surprised at the politics around zoning and development.) After the municipality changed its mind, Casson's friend decided to try again despite losing the investments due to council's dithering. He retrofitted an existing house and created four separate units with communal space, including the kitchen.

"We all put in under $300,000 each for our share of the house and the contingency fund we needed," said Casson. "We spent the contingency money for common furniture for the living room area, for the appliances including two washers and dryers for the top and main floors and for paving the driveway, plus a shared amount that went to the joint savings account for emergencies." They also built an elevator to accommodate one resident with disabilities and the rest of them as they aged. She advises looking into tax deductions for seniors or people with disabilities; they received one that helped lower their bill at tax time.

"Lots of houses in this day and age are big and have a lot of property that could be used for shared living, I believe," she said. Her suite had a living room with a sitting area in front of a fireplace big enough for two wingback chairs and a footstool. Her bedroom was big enough for a large bed, side tables, a television and closets all down one wall, plus her own bathroom. She even had enough space for a walk-in closet. "But I chose to make part of my walk-in closet, which was fairly big, into a little office."

Casson's overall housing costs, including maintenance, dropped because they were split between all the residents. On top of that, they could afford cleaning every single week, which was great as two of them had arthritis in their hands.

Due to the legal agreement, each unit was treated as a share in the house and could be sold separately. Casson lived in the shared space for five years and sold for just under market value, about $400,000. If you're wondering why she sold what seems to be a great space in her preferred neighborhood, it's simple. She bought a house on the lake. She sent me a picture of the sunsets she sees, and yeah, I get it.

## SINGLE SENIORS

Not all single people can afford to do what Casson did, however, especially retirees who have a more limited income. Single women in particular experience a pension gap, which we'll get into later. Dr. Whitzman pointed out that Canada has a dysfunctional housing market, especially when it comes to the growing number of seniors who don't want to move into nursing or retirement homes. It's the same in the U.S. According to an AARP study from 2021, if given the choice, 77 percent of adults over 50 would prefer to age in place, meaning either in their home or moving in with a family member or friend.

One person who came upon a solution to her own housing crisis is Pat Dunn, the founder of Ontario-based Senior Women Living Together (SWLT), an organization that is open to any female-identifying person, 55 years and older, who lives in Ontario. Like others I spoke with, Pat did everything right. She married, had a good job and, apart from a few years out of the workforce so she could spend time with her kids, always worked and contributed to the Canada Pension Plan. She has a partial pension and wasn't frivolous with her money.

Yet, after her husband died more than a decade ago, she found herself struggling to find somewhere to rent and was close to living in her car. She asked me, "How come I was poor?" She went looking for a place to live and it was discouraging, to say the least. The less money you have, the fewer options you have. She looked at rent-geared-to-income senior housing but there was a 10-year wait, and she was already 70 years old. She looked at co-housing options, thinking the cost for a rental would be reasonable. "Well, if they had rentals, they weren't reasonable," she told me. Then she looked at multigenerational places where she could live, pay rent and help babysit kids.

If you're from certain cultures, you're familiar with multigenerational housing. You, your parents, siblings and grandparents live in the same home, and everyone contributes as they can, ideally. Older family members can look after the children while the parents work, and the younger generations can help the older one. Plus, the household is stronger economically, and there is far less loneliness. The concept can be expanded beyond the family unit: Humanitas, Sættedammen and De Hogeweyk are residential and nursing homes in the Netherlands where students live among the senior residents in a co-housing environment. The students generally live for free and interact with the residents. The main ask is to "not bother the residents, which is easy because they're usually hard of hearing." Apart from that, the generations have information to share about what they've learned about relationships, especially the older residents, and they cook together.

The catch with multigenerational living in Canada is that it tends to be family oriented. There are some exceptions like Canada HomeShare, which helps older Canadian homeowners connect with postsecondary students and other adults. What's really cool about it is that if you're 55 and over and you have a spare bedroom in your house, you can rent a space to individuals 18 years and older, including students. Older adults can also rent a room. The program supports aging in place and a safe, affordable space for the renter. And yes, background checks are done.

But Pat felt multigenerational housing wouldn't be a great fit for her. So, she created a Facebook group in 2019 looking for other women to share the cost of renting a space. To her surprise, she got hundreds of responses. She said, "When I started [the Facebook group], I thought I'd be lucky to get 10 women in my local area to chat about living together. The first week I opened [it] up, I had 50 members. By the end of the month, I had 200. I was just dumbfounded. I didn't know what to do with that." Now, SWLT provides resources for women who are looking for roommates so they can rent together even if they're outside of Ontario.

Even with so many applicants, it can be difficult to find the right match. "You're more likely to be successful in these things if you have a willingness for self-examination," Dunn said. "What does it really mean to be like-minded? Because that phrase comes up quite a bit in the Facebook group. [People] want to talk with like-minded women, and I think to myself, 'Well, like-minded about living together or like-minded about the other 100,000 things that you can talk about when you're living together?'"

Things to consider include religion and politics — the two things we've all been told to not discuss. These questions *are* asked when creating a SWLT profile. Other things to consider include food smells and food types. Dunn said vegetarians bring this up in their profiles, some saying that the smell of cooking meat makes them feel ill. If you're a meat eater and you're not willing to stop cooking meat, then you won't be compatible.

People can get discouraged when they start the process of looking for roommates, she explained. "All these variables come up and then they're contacting me and feel disappointed."

Dunn doesn't promise an instant roommate connection but what she does tell interested people is they have to be persistent and work on it. Like anything else, it's about self-examination, understanding that living together is a relationship and that does mean some compromise on the smaller things.

Elle Gallagher, an SWLT member, writes, "Getting to know others, really knowing them, takes time, conversations, laughs, cries and trust. The ones you share community with are not always the ones that come up as your most obvious choices. Lean into this observation. Embrace those who are different."

Dunn said that senior women make great tenants, and private landlords know that. The problem is "they have to still provide an affordable option. Some of the landlords are really kind of neat, and they really do want to help." She told me during our chat that she felt really the problem of affordable housing was caused by the government.

I worry about what will happen to me as I get older. (And please don't email me to say that if I had children, they would look after me. One, that's a terrible reason to have children, and two, there's no guarantee your kids will look after you. Go read the 2008 *Vanity Fair* story on the alleged elder abuse of Brooke Astor or look at what happened to Gene Hackman.) Yes, I have family and friends who I know would help out, but I don't want to burden them (rely on, yes, burden, no), and besides we're all around the same age, plus or minus ten years.

My building has a blend of residents of all ages and, like a lot of condos, is turning into what the National Institute on Aging calls a "naturally occurring retirement" community. That means that every so often, we get visits from ambulances, and people die. It's an odd feeling to walk into your building and have the concierge pull you aside to tell you that your neighbor was found dead in her apartment. The super went to check on her when she didn't come down to pick up her regular medication delivery. That haunts me a bit. Another friend said she's not as concerned about being found dead as she is being injured and not being able to call for help. That's a new fear unlocked.

I had a conversation several years ago with Richard, who worked at the security desk in my building. He suggested that people could put a pair of shoes outside their doors at night and take them inside in the morning. That way, if a pair of shoes remains outside the door well into the day, someone could knock on the door as a wellness check. It might seem ghoulish, but I guess it's better than being found dead a few days later. Nothing really came of the conversation, but looking back, Richard was suggesting a sort of community care.

In an ideal world, I would love to live in a Golden Girls situation, lanai optional. We'd pool our resources, buy or rent somewhere where we all have our own bedrooms with en suite bathrooms. We'd share the communal spaces, and we'd be able to afford in-home health checkups, house cleaning, etc. That way, we would deal with the issues of loneliness, declining health and housing affordability without going into long-term care (LTC).

I'm obviously not the only single person pondering a non-LTC future. Some towns and cities are already taking an urban planning approach to this. In Burlington, Ontario, a Community Wellness Hub opened a few years ago to help older adults remain independent in their own homes with social support and healthcare.

Paul Sharman, a Burlington councillor, spearheaded the program. He witnessed his mother spend her last years in the retirement and nursing home system, which he described as less than compassionate and based on rules, not individuals' needs. He was inspired by a U.S. program called PACE (Program of All-Inclusive Care for the Elderly), which surrounds older adults with the professional help needed to stay at home. There are currently 184 programs across the U.S., and it's expanding. PACE integrates the benefits covered under Medicaid and Medicare. (Though as I write this, I'm not sure what Medicaid and Medicare will look like after the Department of Government Efficiency gets through with them.) PACE also includes services such as meals, hospital and home care, dentistry and adult day care. The pilot Community Wellness Hub in Burlington took a naturally occurring retirement community and upgraded it. "We upgraded the ground floor because it needed to be upgraded anyway," Sharman said. "It was more about creating a decent community circumstance."

He explained that in the U.S., most PACE centers are stand-alone buildings in the middle of communities where there are a lot of seniors, so they're not dealing with people who live in the same building. The Burlington building, Sharman said, "had a large number of older adults in a single place for us to do a pilot project. So, in that sense, we had virtually no changes of any significance." Since there was a high concentration of people whom Sharman described as having multiple acuities and morbidities, having all the resources in place for a captive audience made sense. "A coordinator was working with people in their own homes," he said, "but it's about keeping everybody in their own home because long-term care costs thousands of dollars a month."

This way, people live in their own homes in their own communities with the same budget, which is important for people on fixed incomes. Plus, as Sharman pointed out, it reduces the need for hospitalization, because we're keeping people healthier. It also addresses loneliness: People living in the wellness hub have social activities. Sharman said one of the full-time jobs is coordinating events like daily exercise programs, guest speakers and walks: "The purpose of the coordinator is to look after the wellness of each and every one of the participants." The program is expanding as of late 2024 into Hamilton and London with more integrated teams, which is excellent. I hope it expands nationwide because who doesn't want to age at home where you feel secure and comfortable?

This is just the tip of the iceberg when it comes to living well and aging in place. Let's not forget people with intellectual and physical disabilities, who may also be single, with or without kids. They are disproportionately affected by the lack of affordable housing and are more likely to be unhoused. A lot of charitable fundraising efforts aim to cover their housing costs, but the Government of Canada contributed $800,000 through the National Housing Co-Investment Fund to help build eight affordable housing units for people with developmental disabilities in Toronto.

## CREATING WEALTH WHILE RENTING

Recently, I met up with a few friends for our monthly drinks and dinner, and the conversation turned to the economy because it was March 2025 and we (as in Canada) were being threatened with annexation by Trump (I really want to call him something else but will remain professional) and about to head into a federal election. One friend asked if it made sense to buy a house, explaining that she grew up hearing the cliché that "rent is just throwing your money away." You've probably heard it in the last week or so, actually, from someone older than you who bought their house decades ago. Maybe renting didn't make sense 20 to 30 years ago when homes were affordable, with carrying costs well under the 30 percent of your net income mark.

As Dr. Whitzman said earlier, we've been conditioned to think of our homes as pension and retirement funds. Except, as we know, younger people around the world can't afford to buy homes, which means no opportunity to get that "pension fund." Yet the dream of homeownership still exists for many of us. A 2024 survey done by NerdWallet Canada found that 72 percent of Canadians say homeownership is a priority for them. Their reasons included building equity and it being a good investment.

But is owning a home and paying way more than 30 percent of your income worth it to have a "pension plan" instead of just four walls to live in? How should we be thinking about homeownership these days? I asked Elke Rubach, an adviser and founder of Ruback Wealth, and the short answer is it depends. She pointed out that "the interest in homeownership is because that's the dream that everybody has taught them. Nobody talks about financial literacy in school, but everybody is told that you have to buy a house." It's important to consider *why* you want to buy a home — is it to live in or as an investment?

Plus, it isn't necessarily the easy money it's made out to be. I bought a condo, and I didn't anticipate all the extra costs. I had the deposit, the lawyer's fee and the down payment because I had read about that. But no one told me about home insurance, parking costs if you had a car and how quickly your first property tax payment and maintenance fee would be due. Property taxes will never go down. Mortgage rates fluctuate, and you can end up paying a lot of interest on the money you've borrowed. You may have read that most of your payments go toward the interest on the money you've borrowed in the first five to ten years of your mortgage, and yes, that happens.

Then there's so much money sunk into repairs, especially if you got caught up in a bidding war and didn't get an inspection. The rule of thumb is to set aside 1 percent of your house's purchase price per year for repairs. Another option is to budget one dollar per square foot of your home. Now, this makes sense if you have a massive house, but I can tell you that a 24-inch stacked washer and dryer cost me $1,500, and I do not have a 1,500-square-foot apartment. I wish.

You may sell it at a profit (minus all that money you paid into it), but other houses will have also gone up in price, so when you buy again, you're getting more years with a mortgage or less house than you had before. If you're going to buy a home, do it for the right reason — because you want a place to live, not because you want an asset.

Rubach said that people need to figure out what's important to them and whether it makes more sense to invest in real estate or in the market. "Sit down and figure out what's important to you," she explained. "If you're making ten dollars, it might make more sense to spend three dollars in rent, save three and spend three. That might be better than spending six dollars on home-ownership and having two dollars in reserve if something breaks down. Then you can't do anything because you're beholden to your house." Rubach said that if your rent is close to a mortgage payment, you should run the numbers, including the cost of repairs, property taxes, parking, insurance, etc., to see if it makes sense to buy and get a mortgage. If your rent is lower than a mortgage payment, and you're in a good place and have a good relationship with your landlord, then it may make more sense to keep renting and invest elsewhere. You could also use the price-to-rent ratio, often credited to Campbell and Shiller's model for asset prices. You take the purchase price of a home and divide it by the annual cost of renting a similar place. If the price-to-rent ratio is lower than 15, consider buying instead of renting. If it's between 16 and 20, renting might be a better option. If it's more than 21, renting is better for you, financially.

Too often, Rubach said, people tend to look at homeownership in isolation instead of holistically as part of their overall financial position and cash flow.

Owning a home is a form of forced savings, because you could buy and, years later, sell it at a profit and use that money to buy something else. But there are several issues with that. The first is that if you look at what you paid versus what you sold the home for, there might be a profit, but after you add in all the costs that Rubach mentioned and deduct them from the sale price, you might not come out as far ahead as you thought.

Which leads us to ask, Can you make more money renting and investing than using a house as forced savings? It depends, but there are people who have done it. In *The Wealthy Renter*, Alex Avery advises looking at the average monthly mortgage costs, maintenance and expenses and compare all of that to rent. If there is a difference that advantages the renter, put that amount in investments. This could work well for a young renter who has decades of time in the market. You could also put the money in a first home savings account (FHSA) for a down payment for a future home. The nice part is you get the benefits of the money growing as it's invested and a tax deduction.

The second issue is the assumption that you'll get more than what you paid when you sell it. Property is like any other asset — there's no guarantee it'll increase in value. In bigger cities, if interest rates are favorable to borrowers and the labor market is feeling good about itself, you might. The cities that embody "location, location, location" are more than likely to increase in value. Smaller towns may not see an increase in their property values even after decades because there isn't a demand for them. Your area could also become undesirable due to a change in zoning.

The third issue is you might sell your house for more than you paid for it, but while you were building equity, real estate prices were going up, so you end up buying your new place for close to or even for the same price as the sale amount. My condo is a great example of that. Its value went up, but condos in general have also gone up. I would spend all my money on a new place if I decide to sell and buy again. No retirement savings for me.

While a house can be a form of forced savings (you have to deliver that mortgage payment), if you rent and you have some money available, you can put it in the right investment vehicles for you. Tax-sheltered accounts — like RRSPs, TFSAs and FHSAs in Canada or 401(k)s and IRAs in the U.S. — are especially good places as long as you have contribution room. (Yes, an FHSA is meant to help people save for their first home, but it can help you save toward retirement because you can roll into an RRSP after 15 years if you don't buy a home.) One of the best ways to create forced savings is to set up pre-authorized deposits. On set days of the month, a certain amount is automatically taken from your bank account and put into your retirement account. Just set it and forget it. You won't even miss the money because you never see it.

When answering my friend about whether it would make sense to buy or continue renting, I said she and her spouse should talk to an adviser. Before checking that box on the adulting checklist, we all need to ask ourselves several questions:

- Why do I want to buy a house?
- Will owning a house with the upkeep and costs stress me out?
- Can I afford those costs?
- Does owning make me feel tied down?
- Will renting stress me out because of the threat of renoviction?
- How will I save for retirement if I'm renting?

I also asked her to consider if she wanted housing debt in her sixties and beyond and if that would mean a change in their lifestyle and their ability to save for retirement or do things she liked such as traveling. People may choose to rent or buy depending on their financial situation — and it's not going to make or break your ability to retire.

## URBAN PLANNING FOR SINGLES

I am absolutely not an urban planner, but I can't finish this chapter without touching *extremely briefly* on the topic of urban planning and single people.

First, zoning. Look, Canada's older zoning laws were exclusion-based, targeting people based on income and race. As recently as the 1970s, North York, Ontario, had a zoning policy in place that meant households could only have people related to each other; in 1971, according to *The Globe and Mail*, four women, who were not related to each other, rented a $300-a-month basement apartment. A North York bylaw inspector warned the women within a month of them renting the apartment that they had to move out or face a court case. The women chose the courts. The law was overturned in 1974, after one of the tenants, Barbara Greene, was elected as North York's first female councillor as a result of her fight against the bylaw. Once she was in office, she pushed to have the Ontario Municipal Board review the bylaw. Take a look at that date: 1974. That was not that long ago. There is evidence that similar laws existed in the U.S. In 2022 — yes, you read that year correctly — the Shawnee, Kansas, city council voted unanimously to ban co-living arrangements, which it defined as four or more unrelated adults living together. Kansas isn't the only city in the U.S. with these laws; it's estimated that 25 of the 30 biggest metro areas have a similar law in the books.

Other zoning decisions targeted communities of color such as Hogan's Alley in Vancouver, which was the home of the city's Black community. It was demolished to build a municipal viaduct in the 60s. I mentioned redlining in the U.S. at the beginning of this chapter, but there are other examples of U.S. zoning decisions that disproportionately affected Black communities. In New York City, the city got the Seneca Village land through eminent domain, a law that allows the government to take private land for public use with compensation paid to the landowner. Approximately 1,600 residents, predominately Black Americans, were moved to create Central Park.

In *House Divided: How the Missing Middle Will Solve Toronto's Affordability Crisis*, Cheryll Case, founder and executive director of CP Planning, points out that not much has changed when it comes to housing for low-income women. This demographic is still underrepresented according to the Women's National Housing & Homelessness Network, which found that "women-led households disproportionately live in core housing need, with single parent, women-led households experiencing the greatest need." One reason is the current way community consultations are designed. When the City of Toronto (of which North York is now part) holds a community consultation, the majority of people who show up are "white, male, homeowners and over the age of 55." (Anecdotally, this tracks with my experience attending community meetings.) Even if you're not a homeowner, especially if you're not, it's vital to show up and raise your voice about issues that affect your community. Single people may be able to legally cohabitate, but our interests are still not the priority. Another reason a lack of affordable housing is that urban planning, which includes housing, isn't really undertaken through an intersectional framework. This is not new, and it's not just a North American issue as seen with a 2017 article submitted to Mistra Urban Futures called "Gender Perspectives Often Ignored in Urban Planning," which examined the lack of intersectionality in Cape Town, South Africa, and Gothenburg, Sweden.

So, it was heartening to see a 2024 article in *The Guardian*, "Lens of a Singleton," about Belgian councillor Carla Dejonghe's mandate to transform Woluwe-Saint-Pierre, a neighborhood on the outskirts of Brussels, into the first in Belgium where policy-makers must consider the impact of their actions on those who live alone.

That's because, as I've been banging on about throughout this book, single people bear the full cost of everything. The article pointed out that single people in the UK are out up to £10,000 a year in extra expenses compared to a couple.

Councillor Dejonghe is also the president of all1, an advocacy group for people living alone, and she and her team sent me the paper that informed the policy, *The Political Economy of Single Person Households: How Unadjusted Governmental Policies Affect Singles* by Yelene Van den Bossche, which, by the way, was submitted to research journals in 2015.

I'm not going to recap the entire paper, as it's 55 pages, but here are some highlights:

- Tax reforms were done in Belgium in the early 2000s, and while the results positively impacted couples' net income, reforms barely, if at all, benefited singles.
- It's time to break up with the non-earning spouse allowance, which allows the higher-earning spouse to transfer some income to their partner. The author of the paper pointed out, "In a society where one out of three households consists of a single person, one might wonder whether this measure is still necessary or even justified."
- The housing bonus, which affects the amount of taxes paid, was also unfair to singles. Couples get double the amount compared to a single person, that is, as the author points out, if the single person can even afford to buy a house. (Sounds familiar!)

Councillor Dejonghe's proposed charter has seven recommendations for the municipality:

1. Adopt a single reflex: Always assess policy measures and their impact on those living alone. Strive for measures that are neutral to living arrangements.
2. Consult with the local hospitality and catering industry: There are already a few good examples of restaurants

providing long shared tables for guests who dine alone. More and more businesses also offer good wine by the glass, not just by the bottle.

3. Have more consideration for singletons in the workplace by, for example, raising awareness among staff members to avoid automatically burdening singletons with night or weekend work and off-season holidays.

4. Provide the necessary space to promote social interaction in new housing projects.

5. Aim for accessible and affordable activities for everyone.

6. Eliminate the mandatory titles "Mr. and Mrs." on letters and invitations and allowing invitees to bring a "plus one" instead of a "partner."

7. Involve single residents in policymaking and let them speak for themselves.

It's a start, and as Councillor Dejonghe said in her statement, "For the first time, a municipality is committing to examining its policies through the lens of a singleton." No changes have been made as of writing this, but making policy changes can take awhile. But it can be changed, like that stupid North York bylaw, policymakers the world over, take note.

## THE TAKEAWAYS

- Vote for politicians who have a focus on building affordable housing and strengthening rent control.
- Consider why you want to buy a house. It's not your only option for income generation. Run the numbers using the price-to-rent ratio. Not only will it help you decide what to do, you'll be able to tell your family members why you're choosing to rent or buy.

- Consider options beyond traditional solo living: partner up with friends to buy a place, or explore co-op housing.

**CHAPTER 3**

# Day-to-Day Spending and Saving

If a book about finances doesn't mention budgeting, is it really a finance book? A budget can sometimes feel like a heavy or restrictive thing, but fundamentally all it is is an accounting of and a plan for your money.

Before I get into budgeting, let's acknowledge that budgeting isn't some kind of amazing tool that can solve wage inequality, the housing shortage or miraculously cut the cost of groceries when grocery chains collude to artificially keep the price of bread high for 14 years. What budgeting does is give us knowledge of our own money situation and the ability to make informed choices. Things like the housing crisis, tariffs and food costs are bigger than what our budgets can control. To start to address those issues, we need to vote for people with solid, realistic plans for building more homes and lowering costs. I hope by the time you're reading this book, the tariffs have been consigned to history, but who knows with Trump in office.

With that in mind, how do you create a budget? First, assess your current financial situation. You can do this with a planner, but if you don't want to, there are budgeting tools like the ever-popular Mint (RIP for Canadians), Fina Money, You Need a Budget, Rocket Money, as well as apps provided by banks, but a good old spreadsheet or even a pen and paper can show you if you're earning more than you're spending or vice versa. You don't have to commit to using one of these systems on an ongoing basis if it burns you out, but getting an accurate snapshot is an important starting point. If you're not monitoring your budget on an ongoing basis, check in with yourself at least every three months to see how things are going.

Check your paystubs or bank account and add up your current monthly income (or use a six-month average if it fluctuates). Then add up expenses like your rent or mortgage payment, hydro/electricity, phone, internet, water, debt repayments, food, entertainment, gas and clothes. Then subtract your expenses from your income and look at what's left. If it's less than zero, you're spending more than you make. The bottom line can be a bummer, especially if you're single, but it's not the whole picture. Other things to look at are:

- spending categories that are heftier than you imagined, like dining out or taxis and rideshares;
- spending patterns (e.g., late night online shopping or relying on takeout more heavily toward the end of a pay period);
- "zombie" expenses like subscriptions or memberships you no longer use; and
- service or overdraft fees that you might be able to avoid with planning or a conversation with your bank.

Armed with your new knowledge, you could trim where you can, try to set goals for various categories or try out a particular budget approach. There's the 50/20/30 budget where 50 percent of your net income covers your needs, 20 percent is for savings and the final 30 goes to your wants. There is the pay-yourself-first budget where you pay yourself an amount that covers savings and debt payments, and then you spend the rest on whatever you want. There are budget systems designed for neurodiverse people; some coaches, like Sherry Andrew, who runs Money Mindset Financial Coaching, work specifically with people with ADHD. You aren't beholden to one type of budget or the same numbers every single month. If one style doesn't work for you, try another one. If you need support, there are budgeting coaches out there like Andrew. If you realize you need to increase one area, like retirement savings, you have the numbers in front of you to make conscious choices about where to cut or boost.

During the budgeting process, it's important to know your priorities. Cheapest isn't always best. Between the several jobs that I do, thanks to being self-employed and being single, I don't have much free time these days. When I'm not working, I'm trying to keep my place and myself clean, cook, get enough sleep, exercise, budget, socialize with people, so I don't end up a feral Toronto raccoon, and look after my mental health. I cook and do meal-planning, but I hate the actual act of shopping for food. So, I pay for grocery and meal kit deliveries. Now that's definitely a point of privilege because I can afford to do this, but for me, paying the extra money to get my groceries delivered is worth it. It doesn't mean blowing my budget. I acknowledge that I'm going to spend this money, I factor it into my budget and I don't feel bad about it.

Other people have other priorities: One friend is in meetings from 8 a.m. to 6 p.m. and she wants her lunchtime for herself, so she pays for a dog walker. Others pay for house cleaning. Each of them said that these choices freed up time for them to do things that they actually wanted to do. All these decisions are intentional. Keep in mind that budgeting isn't only about reducing spending — it's also about figuring out how to spend to really make your life better.

## SHORT-TERM SAVINGS

Given the high cost of living for solo earners, maybe spending 30 percent of your money on wants isn't an option; don't beat yourself up — we're not operating in a fair economic system. Start by economizing where you can and focusing on areas where you might need to go harder like putting a higher percentage of your money toward retirement, travel or whatever works for you at this stage of your life.

One thing that should be a priority for all singles, though, is an emergency fund. When you don't have a partner's salary as a financial cushion, it can be very reassuring to have a stash of cash to cover unexpected expenses or a reduction in income (from layoffs, reduced hours, sickness, disability, etc.). You may qualify for unemployment insurance or other benefits, but it may not be enough to cover your expenses, so have a little something somewhere. You'll be glad you have it when you have to call the plumber on a holiday to fix your leaking toilet. *Sighs at $650.* Why do toilets and appliances break on weekends and holidays? It's like they do it on purpose.

Since then, by the way, I've spent $350 to fix a busted outlet and $150 to be told that my 30-year-old stacked washer and dryer had definitely decided to give up, and I needed to spend a further $1,300 to get a new set and about $50 sending out laundry for the month between ordering and installation because this happened during the peak COVID years when everyone was renovating their home and contributing to the supply chain issue. The only appliance that had the decency to die on a weekday was my fridge. It was still $400 to fix, though. I recently had to replace my 15-year-old television with a smaller one that cost $338. Every time an appliance decided to break, I had to tap my small emergency account to fix or replace something.

So, how do you build up an emergency fund in a way that doesn't stress you out? After you've done your budget, look at what's left. Then consider how much you want in your emergency account. The rule of thumb is enough to cover three to six months of expenses, but you may want more than that. If you have less insurance coverage like health, pet or critical illness (more on this later), you'll want to have a heftier emergency fund. Once you've decided how much you want, figure out how much you can spare from each paycheck and set up pre-approved deposits. Start small — they add up to bigger amounts as time passes. When you hit your desired balance, you can reassess and reallocate some or all of that money to longer-term savings. If your income increases, don't forget to increase your emergency account savings.

What if you can't build an emergency fund, though? Then it's important to have a backup plan. Would you be able to live with family or friends for a while? Could you open a line of credit (if you qualify) or add an emergency credit card? Even having a backup plan can provide some reassurance in uncertain times.

Beyond an emergency fund, how much should you save? An old piece of advice was to save 10 percent of your gross salary, but as we'll see in the retirement chapter, that may not be enough for singles (or for anyone in this economy). Ultimately, as a single person, your margins are probably slimmer than a couple's, but even if times are tight, see if you can start by saving a little something. You'll strengthen that habit and build some security, and interest will be on your side.

Whatever you do, automate as much of it as possible, so that your savings comes directly out of your paycheck and into savings and/or investing accounts; you can also pay bills automatically. This automation takes an item off your to-do list, ensures important bills get paid and helps you see how much money you really have available. I'm a fan of having separate accounts for separate goals. Right now, I have savings accounts for property taxes, maintenance fees, gym membership, travel, birthdays (not mine) and ideas, though that one is empty right now because, well, I don't have any ideas that need funding yet. I've set up pre-authorized deposits for all of them and am very pleased when I check on them once a month.

If you have kids or you plan to go back to school, the government will often help support saving for education. Canadians can set up a registered education savings plan (RESP), and the government will kick in some contributions under the Canada Education Savings Grant. The Canada Learning Bond also provides $2,000 to low-income families' RESPs. British Columbia and Quebec have additional education grants. In the U.S., there is the Qualified Tuition Program and 529 plans, tax-advantaged savings plans sponsored by states, state agencies or educational institutions.

## MANAGING DEBT

Debt isn't always a "dirty" word: It's how we fund big purchases like houses and cars or college. And because we live in an unjust economic system, some people need to carry debt just to get by month to month. If you have any kind of debt, ensure you understand the interest rate, repayment timeline and default consequence for each one, especially high-interest debt like credit cards or auto loans. Some forms of debt, like student loans, may qualify for debt relief, like the Public Service Loan Forgiveness program in the U.S. If you have multiple debts, debt consolidation services may help you pay down your debts by combining them, so you make one monthly payment and possibly carry the balance at a lower interest rate.

Generally, you want to pay off credit card debt as quickly as possible because the debt's interest rate is higher than the interest rate on your emergency-fund savings account. Once you've paid off the higher-interest debt, you can redirect that money toward your emergency fund, which should feel pretty easy to do, because you've already developed the habit of saving money. Or you can work on both at the same time, with the smaller amount going to your emergency fund while the larger amount pays down the interest-bearing debt. Once the debt is cleared, redirect the money to the emergency fund with a pre-authorized deposit.

By the way, debt is one area where it can be an advantage to be single: The only person's debt you're taking on is your own.

## HEALTH AND DENTAL

One of the downsides of being single and self-employed is a lack of benefits. I can visit my doctor without paying for it, which is nice, because Canadian healthcare is prepaid through our taxes. (Although several politicians up here are working hard to privatize our healthcare systems because they're horrible people who are interested in profiting from it.)

Americans, I'm sure you know how to navigate your healthcare system better than I do. You probably already know about going to a free or sliding-scale clinic, asking for a payment plan, buying generic medication, double-checking your bills, prescription cards and seeing if you qualify for Medicaid services. If you're not already doing these things, start now.

Sometimes there are discounts to be had with supplemental healthcare. I didn't have dental insurance for a long time and paid out of pocket. I mentioned this to the dental office administrator, and she gave me a 10 percent discount. You can see if there are any dental schools in your region. Your appointment might take twice as long, but you'll be seen by a dental student with a supervising instructor. This also applies to things like massage therapy or even haircuts — wherever there are students training, there are potential discounts to be had. Ask and see what you receive. These days, I pay for an insurance plan that covers about 50 percent of my expenses like dental, eye care and physiotherapy.

In Canada, another option is to see if you qualify for the Canadian Dental Care Plan (CDCP), which was introduced in 2023. According to the federal government, one-third of Canadians do not have dental insurance, and one in four Canadians didn't go to an oral professional because of the cost. You need an adjusted family net income of less than $90,000, to be a Canadian resident for tax purposes and to have filed your previous year's tax return. Signs at dental offices indicate if they accept the CDCP.

I wear glasses and spend money on them since I wear them all the time and consider them to be accessories for my face. While there aren't a lot of savings to be had on eye exams, you can save money shopping for frames. The classic options are to check online or with companies like Warby Parker, Blue Elephant or Gentle Monster in South Korea or JINs and Zoff in Japan. If you need a second pair of glasses for computer work, consider outfitting old frames with new lenses.

## FOOD COSTS

It is straight-up more expensive to eat as a single person, largely because single people tend to buy food in smaller formats. The Royal Bank of Canada crunched some numbers, and one item, milk, was $0.25 per 100 milliliters for a single person versus $0.16

for a couple. That's a singles tax of just over 50 percent on one grocery item. Yogurt was almost 100 percent more when buying in a smaller size.

So, it makes sense that buying in bulk is a frequent recommendation for reducing food costs. But when you're single, it's not a slam dunk. First, who are you going to bulk buy with? The short answer is anyone, though I'd add "with some careful planning." One friend of mine goes bulk shopping with her family. Several do it with their friends. Personally, I do both. My parents have a Costco membership, so when I visit them and we go, I add my items and pay them back. You can also split a lot of bulk purchases, which are often just bundled multiples. Super easy — all the savings without having to eat your body weight in salsa. You could also split a bulk-store membership with someone else — most of them allow two users per "household."

The next question, though, is where to store your bulk purchases if you live in a small space. If you're lucky, you have room for a deep freezer that allows you to squirrel away some of your deals. You might also buy nonperishables with long expiration dates, which can require a little storage creativity. I stash items like shampoo and toilet paper under my bed and on the floor of my closet. But here's the catch: Don't forget you've bought these items, and check in on your goodies every few months.

As for perishables, you may have to be more stringent with what you actually need and use. Before buying something, I calculate how often I'll eat it. For me, if it's a minimum of once a week, then I'll buy, divide and freeze it. It does mean less variety in what I consume, but I know I'm not wasting food. (Wasted food isn't good for the bottom line or the environment, so maybe skip the giant clamshells of greens unless you're a salad fanatic.)

I've cut back on meat to make room in my freezer and budget for other items like frozen fruits and vegetables. These keep much longer than fresh vegetables, so if you're going through them more slowly cooking for one, no food or money gets wasted.

To avoid getting carried away with bulk store bargains, it helps to start by using what you have already: One friend has always been good at using what is in her pantry, looking up recipes based on what she has left. Now she's trying to use everything she has. She also tries recipes in really old cookbooks. There is a stunning amount of Jello recipes; only half of them are kind of disgusting.

I mentioned using meal kits earlier, and while this can be more expensive than some home cooking per serving, it's cheaper than takeout. Because meal kits deliver ingredients in smaller quantities, I can have more variety and I'm not wasting food (and thus money). It's great.

If you're trying to avoid waste, sometimes your diet can get a little repetitive: Enter the meal swap. Meal swaps mean more people can enjoy home-cooked food, and a single person doesn't have to eat leftovers for a whole week. Simply make a big batch of a meal you love (even better if it freezes well), divide it into one-serving containers and then exchange with friends. To make it easy, swap with your neighbors so you're not traveling far with multiple containers. Invite reliable people, and discuss any dietary restrictions and budgets. Are you going to do fresh meals or frozen? Keep the conversation going about recipes, because at some point you may get tired of chili every week, even if it's easy to make. Also, don't criticize someone else's dish; it may have been passed down from your friend's ancestors. The bonus to all this is it makes a great low-cost hangout — food for the body and for the spirit.

Lastly, if you can't make ends meet, look into school meal programs, food banks or community fridges and pantries in your area to help bridge the gap. In the U.S., you might qualify for the

Supplemental Nutrition Assistance Program. There's an unfortunate stigma to this, but food insecurity is becoming increasingly common in our era of wealth inequality and worker exploitation. 13.5 percent of American households were food insecure at some time during 2023. Meanwhile, Statistics Canada reported that 22.9 percent of people in the 10 provinces lived in a food-insecure household. Use of food banks is on the rise: Food Banks Canada reported that March 2024 had its highest visits ever with more than two million visits in that month alone.

These community resources exist to help people and are meant to be used. When things are a little more flush for you, you can always donate time, money or food to those same places and pay it forward. I've sent money to friends who shop for community fridges, and it's so easy. Send them money, they buy food, people eat. And if you're thinking, "Are you sure they're buying food with your money?" Yes, I'm sure. Also, once the money leaves my hands, I don't monitor what is done with it.

## BORROW INSTEAD OF BUY

I do not want a closet of tools because most of the time I need a tool the one time and then it languishes, reminding me that I spent money just to do *one thing*. So, when I need something, I tend to ask friends and family to borrow it first, and if not, I check out options to get something on loan. You probably know you can rent things like carpet cleaners, but stores like Home Depot do tool rentals. Canadian Tire has a Loan-a-Tool program where you put down a deposit, return the tool in its original condition and get a full refund. If you need the tool again, you can keep it, and the deposit is your purchase price.

Many communities also offer memberships to "libraries of things," including tools and extending to other seldom-used and bulky-to-store items like camping and sports equipment, board games and hosting equipment (because you probably won't be using that chocolate fountain on a weekly basis). Instead of buying expensive home items, you buy access to them for a fraction of the price. As tool library enthusiasts like to say, "You don't need a drill; you need a hole in the wall." Some cities also have toy libraries, which not only cuts way back on kid clutter but also ensures that your kids can try new things when they get tired of the old ones.

Regular libraries have also gotten into lending beyond books and other media. The LA County Library lends tools to customers at six of their branches (Compton, Lancaster, Malibu, Norwalk, Rosemead and San Fernando) at no cost. Looking at their inventory, it's a lot: hammers, wrenches, electrical cords, cookware, bike repair kits, sewing machines, gardening tools and power tools. Libraries also often offer free passes to local museums and other attractions, as well as online access to newspapers, magazines and some streaming services, which can lighten your entertainment budget.

Of course, you don't have to have an official membership to borrow something: Buy nothing and free stuff groups have popped up all over the world, filled with people happy to loan something or give it away. They're usually very regional, so you don't have to drag yourself all over the place just to pick something up. Lending someone a ladder is also a great way to get to know your neighbors and help you build community — sometimes the ladder is a gateway to sharing other things like garden produce, childcare, or snow-shoveling duties.

## THE TAKEAWAYS

- Budgeting won't fix inflation or the housing crisis, but tracking income and expenses shows if you're overspending or have money left to allocate to savings or investments. Choose a budget approach that feels manageable and helps you meet your goals.

- Unexpected costs from plumbing disasters to appliance breakdowns can hit hard and inconveniently. Saving gradually, even $10 to $20 a month, can help build an emergency fund without adding financial stress.
- Choosing to spend on services like grocery delivery or dog walking can free up time and reduce stress. The key is being deliberate about these choices and balancing them with cuts elsewhere.
- Buying in bulk can be great, but make sure it ends up in your stomach and not in the compost bin. Be mindful of your storage space and your actual needs.
- Consider borrowing instead of buying.

CHAPTER 4

# Taxes and Spousal Benefits (Maybe Don't Marry Your BFF Until You're 60)

We know there are tax, healthcare and pension benefits for couples, so what's stopping me from marrying a friend for tax or pension benefits, apart from the fraud? The law generally requires "conjugality," but what exactly does *conjugal* mean in this context? Does it mean getting busy on the regular (whatever that means) or at some point, historically, a couple had to have sex?

I went to the source, the Canadian government's website, specifically the page on conjugal relationships. According to the Government of Canada, a conjugal relationship is "one of some permanence, where individuals are financially, socially, emotionally and physically interdependent, where they share household and related responsibilities, and where they have made a serious commitment to one another."

Then it says, "Conjugal does not mean 'sexual relations' alone. It indicates that there is a significant degree of attachment and mutual commitment between two partners."

"Hold on," I said to my friend Kate, who was sitting opposite me in the coffee shop one Saturday morning. "According to the federal government, conjugal doesn't just mean people having sex. So, we could live together and be financially, socially, emotionally and physically interdependent. That means I could, technically, hug you. That would cover the physical aspect. Plus, we've known each other for more than 15 years."

Kate raised an eyebrow at me as I sipped my coffee. "The problem is," I continued, "according to the government, we'd need to have sex probably once."

She squinted at me. "It's not that you're not unattractive, but it'd be like sleeping with your sister."

Why does the government define *conjugal* this way? What if you're asexual and committed to a partnership that is financially, socially, emotionally and physically (to an extent, if at all) interdependent? What if you gave up on sex decades ago?

Well, it turns out you could get married and not have sex to benefit from attribution rules, explained Sabina Mexis, a tax lawyer with Axios Legal. But it's not really worth it. There aren't a lot of benefits to getting married just to take advantage of things like spousal retirement contributions or pension benefits.

"It might make sense if you're 60, but if you're young, you'd have to wait 30, 40 years," she said. Plus, there are several downsides to going this route. You may end up being on the hook for spousal support and splitting the marital home, especially if you bought it together.

So, said Mexis, you could get married, but the downsides are potentially not worth the upside of getting your friend's pension after they croak.

## WHY THE TAX MAN LOVES COUPLES

So how did we get to this couple-focused state? It wasn't always this way. Income tax didn't exist federally until 1917 when it was introduced to help finance the First World War. Even then, income tax "gave special treatment to married individuals despite using the individual as the basic tax unit," according to *Cracking the Conjugal Myths: What Does It Mean for the Attribution Rules?*, a paper by Lisa Philipps.

"Interestingly," writes Philipps, "the federal government was originally hesitant about giving tax recognition to marriage for reasons very similar to those now being cited by the Law Commission." (The Law Commission of Canada published a report in 2001 called *Beyond Conjugality: Recognizing and Supporting Close Personal Adult Relationships* that argued the legal treatment of close adult relationships shouldn't depend on their conjugal nature but on how these relationships support the goals of specific laws.)

When the federal government proposed a basic personal exemption, they did so with no dependency exemptions for spouses, children or anyone else, because they understood that not everyone had those relationships; some people were unmarried and living with siblings or looking after elderly parents.

The opposition thought it was unfair that married men, the majority of whom were going to pay under the new income tax, would not have more exemptions than single people. They even said that it might discourage men from getting married. As a result, the basic personal exemption was cut in half for unmarried people.

Keep in mind that while more women worked outside the home during the war while men served overseas, they were actively encouraged to return home afterwards. Married women who worked in government were actively legislated out of work.

Philipps points out that since then, the definition of *spouse* has broadened from partners only in straight married couples to include common-law heterosexual partnerships, and married and common-law same-sex partnerships.

What hasn't happened is an investigation into why the attribution rules still consider conjugality as the main condition for adjusting taxes and benefits. The Law Commission's report, published in 2001, recommended that the government look at the full assembly of "interdependent relationships between adults." But since then, nothing has really happened with this.

There's only been a little progress on this front, and it came from a surprising place: *M. v. H.*, a 1999 Canadian Supreme Court decision, required allowing spousal support claims by unmarried same-sex partners. This made many in the generally conservative Alberta legislature unhappy. Alberta didn't want to explicitly recognize same-sex relationships, so it enacted legislation that required the courts to consider the issue of when a non-conjugal domestic relationship became entitled to legal recognition.

Alberta's resulting Adult Interdependent Relationships Act of 2003 states "support and other obligations are based on the existence of an 'adult interdependent relationship,' which could be an opposite-sex or same-sex conjugal relationship, or non-conjugal," and it notes that a support obligation may arise after three years in a "relationship of interdependence." That was defined as a "relationship outside marriage" in which any two persons share one another's lives, are emotionally committed to one another and function as an economic and domestic unit.

Thus, one of Canada's most conservative provinces actually did some progressive law-making in 2003, offering platonic relationships some of the same protections as marriage.

## EVOLVING TAXATION

In the months that make up tax season, a flush of articles appear outlining all the deductions couples can leverage. I write several of them every year. But for single people? "The Canadian tax code does not presently provide many, if any, specific tax credits or deductions for single taxpayers," said Warren Orlans, blog editor for TurboTax and a tax expert who spent seven years working for the Canada Revenue Agency. With more Canadians living in a one-person household, is it time for tax breaks for singles to match those given to couples?

Single people in the U.S. also feel the squeeze when paying taxes due to their single status. A married couple can file joint tax returns, getting a bigger tax break compared to singles. For instance, joint filers are eligible for things like a spousal IRA: If you're married and one spouse isn't working, the non-working spouse can contribute to an IRA using joint income. An eligible married couple filing jointly can make IRA contributions to two separate IRAs, or one for each spouse.

Back in Canada, when I asked my single friends what kind of tax deductions they would like to see, one friend, Ilona, said, "I wonder why a couple of siblings can't use the same beneficial tax laws that married couples can, like income splitting." That's where a higher-earning spouse can transfer part of their income to the lower-earning spouse or common-law partner. That can "equalize" their income levels for tax purposes to reduce the tax on the income of the higher-earning spouse.

Couples can also split eligible pension income, such as what you receive from your investment accounts, up to 50 percent with their spouse or common-law partner. If you're in a high-income tax bracket when you retire and your spouse or partner is in a lower one, you can really benefit. Split your income, ideally drop down into a lower bracket and boom, pay less tax.

There is a jurisdiction that acknowledges single people in its tax code. I'm a huge fan of Quebec's restaurant scene and its fashion designers, but you know what I'm also a huge fan of?

Revenu Québec has a non-refundable tax credit for people who live alone or with dependent children — as in no co-tenant, roommate or parents living with you. Revenu Québec states that you may qualify for this credit if you maintain and reside in a dwelling in which you lived alone throughout the year covered by the claim, or only with one or more people under 18 or with one or more of your children, grandchildren or great-grandchildren who were 18 or older and were full-time students. This isn't a measly $100 tax credit. It's a decent amount of money — $2,584 for a single-parent family.

Outside of Quebec, it's not entirely bad news for us singles. Orlans said there are some benefits to filing solo. You won't have to wait for your spouse to file if you're entitled to a GST or HST credit. "When applying for tax credits, such as the GST or HST credit, you don't have to worry that your spouse's income will reduce the amount that you receive," he said. "That's because the credit is based on net household income, so if your spouse makes more than you, you would no longer be eligible."

Tax credits for single people can be done; just look at Quebec. I asked Jami Monte, a CPA and founder of Chillbooks in Toronto, if similar benefits could roll out across the country.

"When we file, we do check off our marital status, and you're right we do file independently even when we're partnered up," she said. "So logistically it should be possible. When I think about the benefits that are paid out based on family income, such as the Canada child benefit or HST credit, they take into consideration if we're partnered up or not, via common law or marriage, when assessing whether we can get paid out."

So, what can we do? Well, as there are more single people every year, we could make it a priority politically. Ask your elected officials or election candidates what they're doing for single people.

Also push to redefine an economic unit. This has been done before when Parliament passed Bill C-23, which gave same-sex couples the same social and tax benefits as heterosexual couples in common-law relationships.

I'm not saying it'll be easy, but there are already reports that have questioned the current attribution rules. The tax code is a living, breathing document (and, as a friend put it, sometimes a hot mess that we dread going near) that should adjust to changing demographics.

Until then, we should max out the tax deductions and credits we do qualify for. You could marry your platonic BFF, but perhaps wait until you're both closer to retirement? Like in a romcom when two friends make a promise to marry each other if they're still single at 40, but make it 60. Or if you don't want to be a romcom star, push for new definitions of economic units that don't require undying love or an agreement made in your late twenties over too many drinks.

## THE TAKEAWAYS

- Know that the tax code moves slowly, but it does move. Push politicians for what you want to see changed.
- Max out all the deductions and tax credits that you can, legally.
- Don't marry your best friend. That only works in romcoms.

## CHAPTER 5

# Entertainment and Traveling Alone: The Pros, Cons and the Archaic Single Supplement

The first time I traveled alone, I went to Japan to teach English. I had flown by myself before but on trips to stay with family or move into a university dorm in English-speaking countries. This time, I wasn't going to stay with family, and I was illiterate. I knew a few Japanese phrases, but I could not hold a complicated conversation in Japanese and I could barely read hiragana and katakana, much less kanji. My support group was on the other side of the world, Google Translate didn't exist yet and Google Maps barely did.

It was one of the best travel experiences I ever had. I lived in Japan for nearly a year, and I really learned how to be by myself and enjoy my own company. Because I couldn't speak the language, I was forced to slow down and take my time; I had to look things up to understand what they were and to make sure I wasn't offending anyone. Tokyo, where I was based, is an old and sprawling city, so I could never hope to see it all, though I did try.

Traveling solo also made me more open-minded. I could have stayed in my room, only making trips to the grocery and convenience stores for food, but I went out and explored the city, went to museums, ate a ton of ramen and karaage in little restaurants, chatted (badly) with the lovely fruit seller on my street who would pull me aside to show me mangoes, went to the movies by myself and had late-night conversations with random strangers (sober and tipsy) on the train as we headed to our homes.

I did make friends, both Japanese and foreign, but those eight months really made me want to travel more by myself. I appreciated not having to worry about or plan with another person.

I'm not alone in enjoying traveling alone: In May 2023, *Travel Weekly* found that tour operators reported a high demand from solo travelers, especially women, and one operator declared it "one of the fastest-growing travel styles right now." In a 2019 study by Travelport, solo travel made up nearly 18 percent of global bookings in the travel industry, and Radical Storage, a luggage storage company, reported a 267 percent increase in online searches for the term "solo travel" between December 2020 to April 2022.

Yet time and time again, single people are denied or forced to pay extra when it comes to entertainment and travel. It's not paranoia if you think you're paying more even though you're consuming less. The UK travel association ABTA analyzed all-inclusive holidays from the country's two largest tour providers and found that solo travelers could pay up to 87% as much more than a traveling pair despite one body in one seat and one body in one hotel room, which would be priced the same if two people were sharing it.

Welcome to the single supplement.

## ENTERTAINMENT AND DINING

The single supplement doesn't just creep up on big-ticket items like hotels or organized tours. It can slide into your daily life. Restaurants can pose a challenge in some countries. In 2023, the Hotel Café Royal in London introduced a minimum spend of £330 for solo diners. The logic is that solo diners take up the same amount of space as two diners but order less. The restaurant says that it does have one or two tables for solo diners where they won't pay the minimum spend, but if you don't get those tables, you'd better come hungry.

Yet solo dining seems to be on the rise. A 2024 survey of over 7,500 diners in seven countries found that 45 percent of respondents sometimes dined alone. In Toronto in 2024, it was up 17 percent, according to reservation booking platform OpenTable. Before the survey, OpenTable wouldn't allow for a single reservation at certain restaurants. "OpenTable doesn't allow one-person reservations for a lot of the fancy restaurants, so you always have to call in and book manually," said a friend who treats her clients with restaurant outings. But when I went on the site and tried booking a single table at some of the more expensive restaurants in the city, it worked. I'm guessing OpenTable pivoted after seeing its own data. If you're not booking online, you might want to call ahead to ensure that a table for one doesn't mean a bill for two.

And if you're worried about being judged for eating out alone, don't be. There is this fear, often called the spotlight effect, where you think you have a giant spotlight on you, highlighting everything you do, say or wear. The truth is people are self-involved and more concerned about themselves than about what you do. So go ahead and eat alone. It's amazing when you don't have to worry about other people, your food and your bill. Savor the freedom of eating alone.

## Bill splitting and other modern plagues

While we're on the subject of dining, there's one last single supplement that can sometimes be inflicted by coupled friends: You're out for dinner or at some sort of event, and you find yourself expecting to evenly split the bill three ways with the couple. But you're not spending as much. Instead of stewing in the resentment, etiquette expert Susy Fossati suggests making arrangements before you sit down or order.

"You could say, 'I'm just going to ask for my bill, if that's okay,' or make up a little white lie such as 'I'm just going to ask for my bill up front, because I might have to leave early.'" She said it's about how comfortable do you feel. "You know, honesty and transparency are always polite, but that's just to each their own right." Personally, I would say I want a separate bill right from the outset, so the server and your dining companions are aware.

Similarly, if you just can't afford an event, it's often best to decline to attend, citing your budget; hopefully with your honesty, good friends will choose less expensive options in the future. If your friends try to pressure you, hold your ground. It's your money. Fossati agreed, adding, "Then change your conversation right away. Talk about that new thing on Netflix. Seriously, move on."

Personally, if this kind of bill splitting happens to me, that's the first and last time I go out with them. I am not subsidizing their meal.

## TOURS AND CRUISES

If you're shopping for tours, all-inclusive vacations or cruises, squinting at the fine print usually reveals that prices are "based on double occupancy." Anyone traveling solo has to pay a bit more than two people sharing the space and the cost.

I reached out to a few people and associations to ask why tour companies charge a single supplement, but I never heard back. (There's a trend here.) I also talked with Shayna Zand, WeTravel's director of partnerships, who has experience with tour groups and the single supplement. She said, "A single supplement gives you your own room at the end of the day." This sounds ideal because sometimes you don't want to share with a stranger who can see your ten-step nightly skincare routine.

"The single supplement is to make up for the fact that yes, you want to go on this group tour, but you absolutely want to have your own room that was priced for two people to share accommodation," Zand explained. The supplement isn't double the price of the trip because it only covers you having your own room, while everything else on the tour remains the same cost. That sounds like it makes sense, but I was still hung up on charging a single supplement on a room. "I'm just trying to figure out the math here," I said, genuinely confused. "If the room was $100 and they're like, 'Okay, we're pricing for two people. So that's $50, we'll add that in.' So do they take that extra $50 and then just roll it on to a single person?"

Turns out tours price the entire trip as a whole, so they have priced the cost of the room and the single supplement for your own room into the total cost. What that means is when a package is offered, because the room is for two, the price per person is usually built in at half the amount. If it's only one person taking up the room, they pay both halves.

That's irritating, to say the least, because the onus falls on the single traveler to shoulder the additional cost, instead of on the tour company, which could figure out ways to be cost efficient or choose accommodation with single hotel rooms.

Solo tour travel can come with other potential pitfalls. My friend Diane booked a trip with her preferred tour company to go to southern Europe, paid her deposit, booked a very expensive nonrefundable round-trip flight and looked forward to beginning her vacation. Then the tour company contacted her to let her know that since she was the only person who signed up for the trip (so far), they would have to cancel and refund her the money for the tour, but not the flight.

Diane was rightly pissed off because the small print of the tour company said that the tour would go no matter how many people signed up for it. "When [the company] contacted me, technically through my travel specialist, they told me I was the only one who'd signed up and were basically trying to get me to change my dates by way of an offer," she told me via email. "I guess because I'd only paid a deposit — even though I was absolutely willing to pay in full. They didn't out-and-out tell me that they'd cancel. But they gave me a deadline to decide. Based on the fact they'd deleted my trip departure from the website and didn't think I'd notice, they were definitely trying to cancel that departure date." Someone else signed up for the tour at the last minute and Diane was able to enjoy her trip, but this incident highlighted that single people have to worry about happenstance when it comes to travel.

Diane shared a tip she learned during this experience that could benefit any traveler:

Sometimes, booking a hotel directly through the hotel's website, rather through a site like Expedia or Hotels.com can be cheaper. One, if they're discounting any rooms, you'll see the most up-to-date price (which might turn out to be better/more accurate than the third-party sites), and two — if they keep their website updated — the hotel's site will show you if there are any rooms available on the dates you want. (I think there's a delay if you go through the third-party sites.) And hopefully, you'll learn about the hotel's cancellation policies — how many days you can cancel in advance (if you need to) without incurring any cancellation charges (or what those charges are, if you fall into the penalty period).

Then there are companies that take advantage of single people. According to a May 2025 investigation by Thrifty Traveler, a consumer travel website, Delta Air Lines, United Airlines and American Airlines were charging a tax on single travelers that almost doubled the fare in one case. Two of the perpetrators rolled back this practice after the report came out.

I took a non-scientific look at whether Air Canada, WestJet and Porter are doing this. When I looked at basic and premium economy ticket costs for single and paired travelers, the prices seemed the same without random price increases. I mentioned this to a friend and her comment was, "They haven't done it probably because they didn't think of it."

It's especially outrageous as solo traveling has increased. According to Yahoo Finance, the travel industry predicts nearly 10 percent annual growth in solo travel through 2030 from all groups ranging from Gen Z to retirees. We're not a niche market.

Whether it's airfare, housing or group trips, being solo often means paying more for the same thing. It's not just frustrating; it's inequitable and unless we keep calling it out, nothing will change. If you see similar pricing discrepancies whether in travel, accommodations or everyday services, document them, share them, and speak up. We deserve transparency and fair treatment. Vote with your money.

Now we have to check if airlines are charging us more when we book our flights. Thanks Delta, United and American for being terrible.

## WAIVING THE SINGLE SUPPLEMENT

Luckily, some tour and cruise operators have realized that single travelers have, well, money. Some have started waiving the single supplement for certain trips, and some don't have one at all. One example is Virgin Voyages, which waived the single supplement for any European trip during summer 2023. Zand said, "When cruise ships have a set number of rooms, a lot of times a single supplement is waived because they need to fill the boat." Sometimes, trips may post a deal early, but in a lot of cases, the deals come closer to the day of departure, so it helps to have a flexible schedule. (Luckily, it can be easier to be spontaneous as a solo traveler.)

### Look for deals

As we've seen, some places will waive the single supplement to fill space. Unfortunately, the onus is on you to find those deals. While it's mostly cruises that seem to waive the single supplement, some tour groups like Overseas Adventure Travel, which was founded in 1978, never charge a single supplement. More women are traveling solo and more tour companies are responding, so be sure to shop around before selecting a tour operator. There's no harm in asking for a deal, but go directly to the head office of the tour or cruise operator. If they won't offer one, consider taking your business elsewhere.

### Understand the math and the language

When you're looking at a trip and you see a price based on "double occupancy" or you see an asterisk next to the price, you can assume that there might be a supplement attached. To figure out the percentage of the supplement, divide the amount by which you'd be overpaying by half of the double occupancy price. For example, if the price for two people is $1,000 (or $500 each) and the price for one person is $600 ($100 more than they're each paying), then you're paying 20 percent more ($100 divided by $500) to have the room to yourself.

### Share with another single

It's not ideal, but share with another solo traveler if you can't afford the single supplement. (Just hope they don't snore. If they do, may I recommend firm, not foam, earplugs and an app that plays 10 hours of white noise. I speak from experience; it works.) It's a valid money-saving tip that's been the common response from the travel industry and agents, as well as personal finance experts. Again, this puts the burden on the traveler instead of on the industry. If they want your money, they should accommodate you.

### Choose the shoulder or off-season

The old advice was that shoulder season, the time just before and after peak travel season, tends to be cheaper, but Zand pointed out that shoulder seasons are becoming more popular and are almost as busy as high season: "Those are the dates now that tour operators are trying to push to combat over-tourism." Deals can still be had in the off-season. While not everything will be open, you can enjoy your trip without a ton of people.

### Look for single rooms

It was a true revelation when I realized that the Ace Hotel in New York City offered rooms specifically for single people. The room was smaller than a standard room but had all the amenities. In late 2024, a single room was US $269 per night (excluding taxes and fees) compared to the larger double-bed room at $369 per night. Imagine what you can do with that extra $100 in New York City. Maybe not much, but $100 is $100.

It's not only the Big Apple. When I went on a vacation to Saint Lucia with two friends, Aya and I shared a room while Grace had a room made for single visitors. We love to see hotels creating space for single people, and pricing it as such. It's more common in European countries due to older buildings and less sprawl. You can also stay at a hostel, where you could share a room.

The cruise industry has started to go beyond waiving the single supplement to designing for singles. According to a press release from 2021, John Diorio, the associate vice president of sales for Virgin Voyages, said solo cabins "are designed and priced for independent travelers, and they perform really well."

As of January 2024, Norwegian Cruises opened up three new solo stateroom categories including Solo Inside, Solo Oceanview and Solo Balcony. Now, we live in a capitalist society and Norwegian is out to profit, so the rationale for these offerings is simply demand. From 2019 to 2022, Norwegian saw an increase in guests booking accommodations as a single occupant in non-studio staterooms. Money talks, and hopefully other companies will embrace solo services in the future.

Until travelers refuse to pay the supplement, certain parts of the industry will continue to charge it. That, thankfully, seems to be changing, and now singles can sometimes travel without the financial baggage of coupledom.

## THE TAKEAWAYS

- Hotels shouldn't be charging a single supplement. If they are, call and ask them to waive it. Take your money elsewhere if they won't waive it.
- Choose travel companies that don't charge a supplement; more tour groups are offering trips that waive it.
- Look for places that specifically cater to single people, with a lower-price single room option.
- Don't let couple friends or any friends guilt you into paying more than you spent on food and drinks. Tell them up front that you're only paying for what you ordered.

## CHAPTER 6

# Insurance:
## Live Your Life, Protected

I once had a vice president of an insurance company tell me that people tend to avoid talking to him about work at parties — it's true that thinking of all the bad things that could happen to us is a guaranteed buzzkill. I told him that I enjoy writing about insurance, especially the fancy stuff like kidnap and ransom coverage that most of us don't need because we're not rich, we don't work in areas where the risk of kidnapping is high or we aren't the beloved family pet. I'm not kidding. A source once told me that a family extended their kidnapping policy to cover the dog. The truth is most of my writing about insurance isn't that exciting, but some of the stories I hear when I talk to insurance brokers and agents are heartbreaking. There's the story one agent told me about a client of his whom he advised to consider getting critical illness insurance. The client didn't, and now he is very sick, not making any income and has a GoFundMe to cover his expenses.

Mundane types of insurance may not be high-octane, but they're way more useful, especially if you're single. A partner can be a sort of financial safety net, and insurance allows you to buy one instead — without a lifetime of listening to someone else's music choices.

If you're single and have no dependents, you may not see insurance as a priority, but one thing that makes a crisis infinitely harder is financial pressure. At best, an unexpected bill is stressful. At worst, it can send you into a spiral of debt. Try to see insurance as buying yourself peace of mind; the news cycle ensures we have more than enough to worry about already.

## LIFE INSURANCE

There are two main kinds of life insurance: term and whole life. Term insurance protects you for a limited number of years, and the premiums are usually cheaper. It's useful if you need money for other things like paying off debt or if you don't plan on leaving a financial legacy. Whole life insurance, on the other hand, provides coverage throughout the life of the insured person. Some policies have a savings component where cash value can build up via interest. When the insured dies, their beneficiaries receive a tax-free lump sum of money.

"Just because you're single, it doesn't mean you don't have dependents," said Gabriel Lalonde, a certified financial planner at MDL Financial Group in Ottawa. That includes single parents obviously, who want to provide for their children, but he pointed out that you may have siblings, parents, other family members or even pets who are dependent on your income.

If you're thinking of getting life insurance, jumping on it sooner, while you're healthier, is smarter. Your family's health history can also factor into your premiums. "It might be worthwhile to lock in for insurability now [before] you're ever diagnosed with something that [makes it] near impossible to get insurance [in the future]," Lalonde explained. "You're also benefiting from lower prices because the price is never going to get cheaper than today." Statistically speaking, the younger you are, the lower your insurance premiums.

Lalonde said that one reason to have insurance as a single person is that it can cover things like funeral or housing costs while your estate goes through probate — that money is accessible more quickly.

If you're a high earner, life insurance could do more than provide security for your beneficiaries. Lalonde said, "If they've maxed out their TFSA and RRSP and they're looking for another way to grow money tax-free, that's where you get permanent life insurance as an option." The cash within the policy accumulates interest that is tax-free until you take it out. Gabriel said it can help you diversify your overall portfolio, and you can borrow up to 90 percent of the cash value in the plan. Now some of these loans aren't interest-free, but as long as you're paying off the interest when you pass, the death benefit and the cash values go to pay back that loan, and then the remainder is paid to your beneficiaries. Banks don't mind these kinds of policies because the cash value in the policy continues to increase, so they know they'll get their money back when the holder dies.

If you're a business owner, life insurance can help your business continue after you die. "There are a lot of single people who are business owners," said Lalonde. "So if you die, and you've got a key role in the business, that is going to cause a big disruption." The money from the policy can be paid to the business and used to hire someone to replace you or to pay capital dividends. That means the money doesn't have to come out of the company, which reduces the disruption resulting from your death. Your executor or business partner won't have to scramble to sell the business, and your death won't have a big effect on the business's day-to-day dealings.

Finally, a life insurance payout could save the family cottage, if your family has one and it's important to you. The money could cover the cost of the capital gains tax from transferring the property, whether in Canada or in the U.S.

## CRITICAL ILLNESS AND DISABILITY INSURANCE

Years ago, I met my insurance agent at a Toronto Starbucks to discuss critical illness and disability insurance. He suggested I should have both since I was single and freelancing. To this day, I remember him going through what my critical illness policy would cover. He said that it would cover 26 illnesses including the big three: cancer, stroke and heart attacks. He started listing the other 23 illnesses like multiple sclerosis, Parkinson's and paralysis until I asked him to stop because . . . yikes.

Critical illness insurance gives you a one-time predetermined lump-sum payment if you get diagnosed with a covered medical issue. Even if you have health insurance that covers treatment and medication, you may be faced with bills for equipment, supplies or complementary therapies. We have universal healthcare in Canada, but it doesn't cover everything, and getting sick is expensive. In 2024, the Canadian Cancer Society reported that cancer costs patients an average of $33,000. (It's about $150,000 in the U.S.)

Disability insurance, on the other hand, replaces a portion of your income for a specified time if you can't work temporarily or permanently due to illness or an accident. Generally, it replaces 60 to 70 percent of your income. It can help you pay your bills while you're sick without draining your savings. Neither of these insurance payouts need to be paid back.

It's a good idea not to just set it and forget it with insurance; revisit your policies as your circumstances change. Several years after I got my critical illness and disability insurance policies, my insurance agent and I were doing our annual check-in. He asked me if my mortgage had increased, and it had. After looking at the numbers, I decided to up the coverage on my disability insurance so that my mortgage and maintenance payments would be covered if anything happened to me. I still worry, but at least I'm covered.

## OTHER INSURANCE

There are other types of health insurance to consider. One example is short-term health insurance, which bridges the gap when you're uninsured. This one seems specific to the U.S., and especially useful if you've missed the open enrollment period for Affordable Care Act insurance plans.

Another is travel and medical insurance. I never travel without it. The last thing I want is either a massive bill if I get sick in America (when I used to travel there, which since 2025, nope) or to stress my family figuring out how to bring my body home in a worst-case scenario. Costs vary depending on your health situation, but I personally wouldn't travel without it.

Travel insurance covers flight delay costs, such as food and accommodation between the cancellation and the next available flight. For trip disruptions such as canceled or cut-short trips, you may be entitled to a full or partial reimbursement of flight or hotel costs. It also covers theft or misplacement of your luggage and other personal belongings. Like home insurance, travel insurance can cover you if your actions cause damage to another person's belongings or property. If something happens to you like a medical emergency, it can cover hospital and dental bills as well as the cost of medical evacuation back home or to another hospital. Some travel insurance will cover the cost to repatriate your body if you pass away while traveling.

Travel medical insurance puts the focus on health coverage, not travel disruptions. It's for people who are planning to live or work abroad for an extended period. They may not get health coverage in their new country and will not be able to access their home country's health plan, so they need insurance to replicate the coverage they would get at home. Travel medical insurance, also known as international medical insurance, covers the following, depending on your policy:

- doctor's visits;
- prescriptions;
- dental;
- vision;
- emergency services like ambulance rides;
- hospitalizations, surgeries, tests, etc.;
- physiotherapy;
- rehabilitation;
- pre-existing health conditions;
- evacuation or repatriation back to your home country;
- treatments such as radiation and chemotherapy; and
- mental health care.

Since this insurance policy is health-focused, you may have to submit your medical history or be examined by a doctor as part of the application process. Since this policy doesn't have a set end date, you may have to pay monthly or yearly premiums.

**Home and tenant insurance**
You have valuable things in your home, and you should protect them. Most financial institutions require you to have home insurance if you want a mortgage. Home insurance protects you, your visitors and your personal items. Coverage includes damage to your home, theft or damage to your personal items, injury to others that occurred in your home or on your property, accidental damage you've caused to someone else's property and personal

property stolen from your vehicle. You might also see home insurance referred to as property insurance.

Be aware that home insurance only covers what's outlined in it, or "named perils," unless you purchase comprehensive home insurance. Regular home insurance won't cover everything that could happen to you and your home, nor is it meant to help with day-to-day home maintenance. So, unless you buy insurance for hurricanes, flooding and fire, you may not be covered. Even then, your insurance policy may not cover everything. Some owners whose homes were affected by the 2025 L.A. fires found that their insurance did not cover damages from the toxins generated by the burning and smothering of the fires.

Tenant or renter's insurance is very similar except since you're not the property owner, it doesn't cover the physical building, just your belongings and if anyone is injured in your space.

### Pet insurance

Furry, feathered and scaly friends and family can be expensive, and most of the time they can't tell us what's wrong. Vet visits and medication are pricey, so pet insurance can be useful, but it's a good idea to read the fine print. When you go searching for what pet insurance covers, you'll see that it's good for things like surgery or emergency situations but generally doesn't cover common costs like extractions, spaying or neutering or regular checkups. Plus, most policies are reimbursements, which means you have to pay up front, then make a claim. It might be a good idea to put away some money monthly to cover those charges.

## THE TAKEAWAYS

- Consider the type of insurance you need to replace your income in the case of an accident.
- The younger and healthier you are, the lower the premiums are for life and health insurance in general.
- If you have dependents, consider life insurance so you can keep taking care of them after you're gone.
- Meet with your broker or agent once a year to see how much insurance you need to maintain your lifestyle.
- Always have travel insurance and consider travel medical insurance.
- Read the fine print of all your policies.

## CHAPTER 7

# Wills and Estate Planning
# (aka Your Last Chance to Be Petty)

No one really likes to think about estate planning because there's this vibe that doing your will + estate = you dropping dead right after you sign them, and no one likes to think about death. But having an updated will, power of attorney and estate plan is especially important when you're single, and even more so if you are estranged from your family. Having a will means they don't get your assets. It sounds petty, but if pettiness gets us to take action, I'll take it.

Nearly half of Canadians and two-thirds of Americans don't have a will. Are you really going to let other people determine what to do with your assets, kids, pets and favorite things after you're gone? Or, possibly worse, let government formulas decide?

Estate planning can be empowering, because it allows you to make sure the right people get your things and money, your correct name and gender are used, your pets don't have to go to a shelter and your life is celebrated *how you want*. Generally, we can't control when death comes, but we can control what happens after.

Having these documents helps everyone, obviously, but there are some unique benefits for some people. For some members of the 2SLGBTQIA+ community who face a lack of support from bio-family members and discrimination from many institutions, having an estate plan can help them outline their health and financial decisions while they're alive and well. Transgender individuals should have an updated estate plan that affirms their name and gender so they don't get deadnamed or misgendered during treatment or even after death. Yet a CIBC poll done in 2022 found that only 39 percent of 2SLGBTQIA+ Canadians have a legal will — even lower than the 50 percent average across all groups. After fighting to be yourself in life, don't give this up in death or sickness.

All the experts I speak with when I write about this subject say the same thing: People get really weird and emotional about money, especially inheritances. Let your final act of love be making things easy on your loved ones as they grieve. One friend said years ago, "My granny had her entire funeral planned out for the family, down to even the bagpiper who would play for her service. The family was blessed with the ability to literally walk into the funeral home and say, 'We need to activate the funeral plan for Casey,' and I think that was pretty much it besides dealing with paperwork. Considering she died somewhat suddenly, I thought it was a blessing. I know that level of planning is rare, but I wish it for everyone."

Let's get into the tools that can help you be closer to Casey.

## WILLS

A will is the legal document that tells your chosen executor (your legal representative doing your postmortem paperwork) what will happen to your assets and property after you die. "It disposes of your property in the manner of your choosing," said wills and estates lawyer Robin Hammond. The freedom to give away your assets as you wish is, as Hammond noted, limited by law, which may give people in certain relationships to you (e.g., married spouses, some family member dependents) a claim to part of your estate. I won't get into too much detail, but in the 2022 case of *Pascuzzi v. Pascuzzi* in British Columbia, a man left his entire $1.8-million estate to his new wife. B.C. Supreme Court Justice David Crossin ordered 30 percent of the proceeds to be paid to the man's 32-year-old daughter from a previous relationship. That can happen in B.C. and in Alberta, but it is a bit harder to do in the rest of Canada. Now, any will can be contested, but one, it takes time; two, it takes money; and three, neither of those guarantees success, especially if the will has been properly created and notified. Plus, if you do win, you might not see any of that money because you spent more than what was in the estate on lawyers' fees.

When you die without a valid will (known as intestacy), the laws of your region (state, province, territory, etc.) determine who has a right to be your estate trustee, as well as who shares in your estate and in what portions, Hammond said. In Ontario, for example, when this happens, the Succession Law Reform Act kicks in to determine how your estate is distributed. Basically, your closest next of kin gets it, even if you don't like them. In the state of New York, order of succession is spouse, children, parents, siblings.

Only married spouses, blood relatives and legally adopted children are automatic beneficiaries of your estate under these laws. Common-law spouses are not recognized as automatic beneficiaries, although they may apply to the court to be your estate trustee or make a claim on your estate in court. These laws say that if you aren't legally married and you don't have any family, even remote family, your estate becomes property of the government.

If you aren't satisfied with the way the law will divide up your estate, you need a document to tell them what to do instead. This is often the case for single people who have important relationships that they want to recognize that fall outside marriage or blood ties. Erin Bury, cofounder of online will platform Willful, explained a will puts you in the driver's seat: "It doesn't leave it up to that provincial formula, and when you're single, you may be really apt to give something to a charity if you don't have children. You might really want to leave something to a really close friend, and that also wouldn't be accounted for in the formula."

Some single people feel strongly about excluding blood relatives entirely in favor of their chosen family, and a will can often achieve this goal, since it's time-consuming, expensive and often difficult to overturn. A will may also offer some of the same advantages to single people as it does to spouses, such as tax- and succession-planning strategies for people who have business interests.

### What should a will cover?

At minimum, a will names your estate trustee and sets out who benefits under your will and how, in legally tested language. However, there are many important details that a professionally drafted will includes to make your intent clearer and to make it easier for the estate trustee to complete your instructions. It can also include powers and clauses that allow the estate trustee to make the most of your assets from a financial perspective, like how they can invest your assets and create tax efficiency.

Choose your estate trustee or executor carefully, and whatever you do, please ask the person if they want to be the executor of your estate. It's a big job that includes:

- finding your will;
- arranging a memorial that you want (Just like Casey who knew exactly what she wanted. Party? Absolutely. Bagpipes, maybe not, but steelpan or your favorite

musical instrument, definitely. Nine-day wake? Go forth.);

- finding all your assets and liabilities and inventorying them;
- paying any bills;
- communicating with beneficiaries and lawyers;
- contacting banks, credit unions and insurance companies to cancel and close credit cards and accounts;
- terminating driver's licenses, passports and health cards;
- closing phone, internet and subscription accounts;
- figuring out pensions;
- arranging for the cleaning and sale of primary and secondary residences and changing the locks, if necessary;
- filing your final income tax return and getting the tax clearance certificate or equivalent; and
- keeping detailed records of all expenses paid and received by the estate.

They may also have to deal with your digital assets, including your email, social media platforms, letters, photos, cryptocurrencies and NFTs, even if they're pretty much worthless. That's why Jackie Porter, a certified financial planner and adviser with Carte Wealth Management and owner of Team Jackie Porter, highly recommends documenting your passwords in a side drawer and sharing your information with your lawyer or a trusted contact. You can also use a password protector, but remember to tell someone your primary password before you die or no one will be able to access your accounts. Hence the literal paper trail in the side drawer. (Maybe make it the other side drawer, if you know what I mean.) Executors can be so overwhelmed that Porter launched another business, the Legacy Toolbox, to organize people's documents in both a physical and digital package.

Being an executor can be a thankless job, especially if you leave them a mess to clean up. One friend was an executor for a couple and spent months fighting a vacant home tax on one of the apartments owned by them.

Your will should also clearly outline what your beneficiaries get from you including investments, cash, property, jewelry, furniture, art and clothes, maybe even down to the plants in your garden. You may think I'm kidding, but I interviewed someone who told me about three sisters who fought over who would get their mother's prize peonies.

By the way, if you are single and leaving something to someone, especially an extended member of the family, let them know. There was a *Wall Street Journal* article in 2024 about the rise in surprise inheritances due to more and more single people without children. Giving people a heads-up can help prevent the drama that inheritances often bring. Unless you want them to live an HBO drama.

You can distribute your estate in one of two main ways: by spelling it out as a specific request ("I give X person the specific thing or the specific sum of money") or as a share in the residue — what's left after all debts, taxes and bequests are paid. It all depends on how you want to distribute your assets to your family and friends. If there are specific items you want specific people to get, spell that out. Specific bequests ensure certain people receive the particular items or sums, but that doesn't work if the asset no longer exists or the estate lacks liquidity. A residual share, on the other hand, adjusts to the estate's final value, ensuring fair distribution but without guaranteeing any one beneficiary a fixed amount. Many people use a combination of both to balance certainty with flexibility. You know your beneficiaries best.

Wills also often include trusts. In very simple terms, a trust is a legal document that has your wishes for how and when you want to transfer assets to the recipient. There are different types of trusts and they can be complicated: trusts to benefit minors, like your kids, and maybe control those assets beyond the age of majority; trusts to benefit persons receiving government financial support who would lose entitlement to that support if they inherited directly; or trusts to benefit people who would burn through the money if they inherited it directly (spendthrifts). Work with a lawyer, please. One of the benefits of a trust is that trustees can manage it if the client becomes incapable, since a trust has a governance mechanism in place to make those decisions.

## Guardianship of dependents

If you're a parent with minors who depend on you, name a guardian for them if you die. Even if you're co-parenting with your ex or partner, both of you should do this in your wills, specifying your wishes like requesting that your children do not go to your parents or siblings but instead to your co-parent's sibling. It's not legally binding, but it can strengthen your case and position. The courts will be aware of your wishes when it comes to your children and consider it as part of their final decision.

By the way, if you have dependents with four legs and a tail, or a shell or feathers, you can make sure they're cared for too. Bury said that pets are a big part of wills, at least for people who choose Willful: "Their pet is really the most important thing to them, so with a will you can leave money for their care. Even if you have a cat, leaving a couple thousand dollars for their vet bills or food in the will is helpful." One of the top reasons pets end up in shelters, she said, is their owner passes away without making a plan for the pet's care, and nobody claims the pet. So it ends up in a shelter. Don't do that to your furry friend. They don't deserve that.

## Guardianship of people with disabilities

If there is someone in your life who will need support after you're gone, arrangements for their care should be in your will. A legal guardianship, set up to deal with financial and personal care matters on their behalf, should include trusted people to look after and support them in all ways.

Things to consider include designating a legal representative to manage the money that comes from a registered disability savings plan. That could amount to hundreds of thousands of dollars by time the beneficiary reaches 60 years old. If you are the parent, remember to designate someone. In the U.S., there are ABLE accounts, which are tax-advantaged savings and investment accounts for individuals with disabilities. Another thing to consider is how an inheritance may affect the beneficiary's ability to receive benefits. Most provinces and states have an income threshold, and if a person exceeds it due to an inheritance, they lose access to government benefits including things like free classes and transportation. You can speak with a lawyer about how to set up your will in a way so your dependent could receive their inheritance without losing needed government support.

## Can you change your will?

Once you make a will, you might wonder if you can change it. The answer is yes: In fact, you should update it if anything major in your life changes. But also: Can you disinherit a beneficiary who is listed in your will, aka cut them out (as so many parents threaten to do, jokingly or not)? Yes, but under very narrow circumstances. Canadian courts generally do not consider sex, gender or religious beliefs to be valid reasons for disinheriting someone.

In the U.S., you can also disinherit people and the same general rules apply. Different beliefs about sex, gender, politics and how to raise children have all been used as reasons for disinheritance, and most of the time they don't fly. You can disinherit a person if they stole from you. That's a very simple explanation, but consult with a lawyer if you plan on leaving out a beneficiary.

If you're newly single, changing your will is a must. The one mistake people make, said Bury, is forgetting to update life insurance, retirement accounts, pensions or any accounts that have a beneficiary name directly on them. "They don't give a shit if you were divorced," she said. "If your ex or your parents are named on the account, they're getting that life insurance payout." Updating your will alone isn't enough: Remove your ex from your life insurance policy, your retirement accounts and any joint bank accounts that you have. If you passed away without doing so, those joint assets would transfer right over to them.

## Costs

Wills aren't just for rich people or even the middle class. Cost shouldn't be a big barrier to making a will. Now, the more complicated your financial and family situation is, the more it can cost, but there are options for most budgets. DIY will kits are the lowest cost option, ranging from $50 to $200 and available from places like Staples, LawDepot, Rocket Lawyer, TotalLegal, Trust & Will and Willful. Working with a lawyer can cost between $300 to $1,000, with the average cost being $624, according to Willful.

A lot of these kits have clear, comprehensive questions to help you articulate your decisions, and you can definitely use them if your estate is pretty simple. (Don't be tempted to use AI, which can use inaccurate and out-of-date information.) But there are benefits to using a lawyer. They have years of experience, understand the nuances of your situation and are covered by malpractice insurance should any mistakes happen. They also offer the assurance that your wishes will be carried out. An incorrectly drafted will could cost your estate thousands of dollars in legal fees if your will is disputed. That's money that won't go to your beneficiaries, and your assets could be tied up in legal action for years, draining your estate.

## POWER OF ATTORNEY FOR PERSONAL CARE AND PROPERTY

When I set up my power of attorney (POA) for personal care and property, I told my brother that now he could theoretically sell my condo out from under me. He said that I could do the same thing. It's a good thing we like each other as people, not just as relatives. We laughed, but it does highlight why you should have a POA and why you should choose someone you trust. People with power of attorney privileges can make healthcare or financial decisions for you while you're still alive but incapable of making your own decisions. You can separate the healthcare and financial roles if you'd like, and sometimes healthcare is completely separate and covered by advance directives. No matter your age, you should have a power of attorney in place because you never know what could happen. *Attorney* in this case doesn't mean an actual attorney; it means choosing someone you trust like a family member or friend. (Though you could choose a professional attorney, who would perform this role for a fee.)

There are several types of powers of attorney, and the names and requirements for them vary based on where you live; review the particulars for your specific province, territory or state. If you don't have these in place, those who end up making decisions for you could be guessing at what you want at best and not looking after your interests and well-being at worst.

## MEMORIALS

Back to Casey and her memorial plan. You can use your estate plan or end-of-life plan to have your say on your final event. This is where you can state what you want done with your body: cremate, entomb, turn into a diamond, body farm donation, etc. Specify things like if you want to be an organ donor because your family may be in shock or too grief-stricken to remember your wishes. Also consider if you want a funeral and/or a memorial service. Do you want to leave a message for people during the event? Do you want an obituary published, and if so, where? Finally, you could take this opportunity to make sure that certain people don't get to come to your send-off. You see? There are so many satisfying ways to be petty from beyond the grave.

## THE TAKEAWAYS

- Have an estate plan, including a will and a power of attorney, so you have final say in your care while you're alive and your finances after you're gone.
- Make sure any dependents are taken care of in your will.
- Have your say on how you want your assets to be shared and how you want to be remembered. Want a massive weeping angel built over your grave? Save up the money, and put that wish in your will.
- Be specific with your wants.
- Update your estate plan once a year or after a major life event.

## CHAPTER 8

# Retirement
# (Because You Don't Want
# to Work Full-Time Forever)

I'm obviously not the only person thinking about retirement. Do I expect to entirely stop working and just do something else? Probably not, as I told a friend one day, because I'd need more than one hobby to occupy my time. I can see myself doing some writing in the future, traveling and continuing my Spanish lessons with the hopes of vacationing in Spain and other Spanish-speaking countries. I dream. I have friends who straight-up tell me that their plan is to work until they die. That's even more likely to be your plan if you're single — but it's an avoidable fate, especially if you start planning early.

In this chapter, we'll get into your burning questions like: Can a person retire on a single income? Can you live on a government pension alone? How much do you actually have to save for retirement? Is saving 10 percent of your paycheck for retirement enough for single people? Can I just go to bed and not think about any of this? Or, as a source asked me for an article about Gen X retirement, "Like, will I have to create a side hustle to spice up the flavor of my cat food?" (Why is it always cat food we're reduced to eating in situations like this? Anne Kadet of the *Café Anne* newsletter republished an old story in her April 2024 issue about how she ate dog food for seven days. Long story short, she got some decent health benefits, but no one, including vets and nutritionists, thought it was a good idea.)

Let's take a look at the why, how and what we can do to save for our future retirement, whatever that looks like.

## RETIREMENT BENEFITS FOR COUPLES

But first . . . couples. Before we get to what solo earners can do, let's note the leg up that couples have when it comes to retirement.

- A couple can split the higher-income earner's pension income when they're both retired. In Canada, this includes the registered retirement income fund (RRIF) after the age of 65, and in the U.S., Social Security. That means less taxes paid on the withdrawal of retirement savings and more money for the couple.
- A couple can combine tax credits on donations and on medical expenses, so they get a larger reduction of their taxable income.
- In Canada, the higher-earning partner can contribute to the lower-earning partner's RRSP. The higher-income partner gets the tax deduction while their partner has sole access to their RRSP in the future. A couple can focus on one RRSP and get a higher tax refund, and that money could be put toward the other's RRSP. The U.S. has something similar with spousal IRAs, where the working spouse can contribute to the non-working one's IRA.
- Most pensions with survivor benefits are paid to surviving spouses. Some may have survivor benefits that pay out to children or to an estate. A Canada Pension Plan (CPP) survivor pension is paid to the spouse or

partner of the deceased owner of the plan. When you're single, even if you're living with a family member, you don't benefit from survivor pensions.

This is the part where I once again point out that this system is outdated, considering that there are other economic household structures that exist beyond spouses. Remember the two sisters from the beginning of this book? They're an economic household, and they should get survivor's benefits.

## MAKING YOUR MONEY MULTIPLY

One of the most common ways to multiply your retirement savings is none other than investing. Investing can seem scary, especially if you don't speak finance. As inflation rises and prices go haywire, it's especially important that your money makes money — compound interest is a magical thing when it's working for you. Luckily or unluckily, depending on your choices, getting involved in the stock market no longer requires specialty knowledge or reading the business section every day, but there are a few basics you should know before investing.

First, understand your investment products and associated fees. Understand the basics of stocks, bonds, exchange-traded funds (ETFs) and mutual funds and what kind of account you're keeping them in. Will you get a tax deduction when you deposit money? Usually, it makes sense to prioritize investing inside tax-protected accounts, such as RRSPs or 401(k)s. Will you be taxed when you withdraw from that retirement account, and how much? If you're using an adviser, are you paying a fee for advice, or do they take a percentage of your assets under their management? You also may want to know what you're investing in — or what you're *not* investing in. There are lots of funds that screen for things like investment in tobacco, weapons and fossil fuels. Most major banks or investing platforms have socially responsible funds; environmental, social and governance (ESG) funds; or halal funds.

Second, know your own risk tolerance when it comes to investing. How much are you willing to lose within your portfolio? For example, if you stayed (reasonably) calm and didn't look at your investments from mid-February to mid-March 2020, you may have a higher risk tolerance. Multiple factors contribute to risk tolerance such as your time horizon (how much time you have before you need to use that money), your future earning potential and your other assets like a home or a pension. While the market has historically trended upward, there have been some notable dips, and of course, nothing is guaranteed.

Third: Diversify. Diversifying means spreading your investments over different asset classes (stocks, bonds, cash, etc.), regions and industries. Not putting all your eggs (no matter how expensive they are) in one basket. There's a reason the financial industry likes to mention this constantly: While it doesn't prevent loss, it should make it easier to weather the inevitable financial storms. Even when markets dropped early on during the pandemic, not all industries were affected equally.

Finally, as we discussed in chapter 1, talk to an expert. Or you could use a robo adviser, such as Vanguard in both Canada and the U.S., Betterment in the U.S., or Questrade or Wealthsimple in Canada. I like them because for a small management fee, they'll keep your money in automated diversified portfolios and adjust as necessary, which is great for hands-off investors. They're also good for new investors who are looking for low fees and easing their way into investing. They have several types of portfolios and you can choose the best one for your needs after you answer a short questionnaire about your money, risk tolerance and time horizons. If you have a lot of assets invested in different spots, a robo adviser can't give you the big picture, though, and a human might be an important part of your financial planning. Advisers can also offer emotional support when the markets do something outrageous or you're stressed about your financial future.

As you get closer to retirement age, you'll likely want to adjust your investment plan. You might want to pay off high-interest debt so you're not carrying unnecessary costs that eat into your retirement income, and you might shift your investments to protect your money while keeping some growth to outpace rising costs.

In Canada, max out your TFSA and RRSP contributions to get the most tax advantages. If you have a pension, confirm eligibility, amounts and payout options. Six months before you retire or the year you turn 71, whichever one is earlier, update your beneficiary details and apply for CPP and Old Age Security (OAS). (You can start your CPP as early as 60 or as late as 70; if you wait to cash in, you'll receive a larger amount per year.) Lock in supplementary health insurance if needed.

In the U.S., there are a couple different things to take advantage of: According to William Bevins, a private wealth manager at Cypress Capital in Nashville, people over age 50 are allowed to make additional contributions to their retirement accounts. The additional contributions help soon-to-be retirees catch up on their retirement savings. He said the amounts vary from US $1,000 for traditional IRAs and $7,500 for 401(k) and 403(b) plans.

If you have a choice of where to put your funds, Herman Thompson, a financial planner with Innovative Financial Group in Atlanta, suggested focusing on the traditional 401(k) because it provides a deduction for both federal and state taxes, depending on where you live. "So, if they're about to retire in places like Florida, Texas, Tennessee or Nevada, they don't have a state income tax," he said. "If you're in a high-income-tax state, like California and New Jersey, or even a moderate-income-tax state like Georgia, and you end up retiring in one of these sunny climates that doesn't have a state income tax, you just made anywhere from 5 to 10 percent of your taxes just disappear forever by using the traditional 401(k)."

Another thing a person can do to catch up is to make nondeductible IRA contributions, said Bevins. He explained that the funds within the IRA would experience a tax deferral until you take it out, when it's taxed. The other maybe-not-great aspect is you won't get the tax deduction, as the name says. "Also, buying index funds with a long-term goal in mind will help grow wealth outside of the qualified plans at very low costs."

He said that the key to maximizing retirement savings is education: "There are many different plans with ever-changing rules. It is important to stay on top of the type of plan(s) someone currently participates in. If you understand how your plans work and what is and is not allowable, you're doing yourself the largest favor in the world." If not, check in with an adviser. That's what they're there for.

## PENSION INEQUALITY

Most people will receive some kind of government pension — unfortunately, some receive a lot more money than others. For example, Canadian women still don't have pay equity, according to Ontario's Pay Equity Office, which affects their ability to have a stable retirement. A May 2024 report called *Understanding the Gender Pension Gap in Canada* found that women fare less well than men during their retirement years, and the situation hasn't improved since 1976.

In fact, it's gotten *worse*. The gender pension gap was 15 percent in 1976, and despite women's increased participation in the labor force, it widened to 17 percent in 2021, according to Statistics Canada. The average retirement income for Canadian women in 2021 was $36,700, and the median was $29,700. "Women receive $0.83 to every $1 a man receives in retirement income. That is a 17 percent gendered pension gap," Kadie Philp, commissioner and chief administrative officer of the Ontario Pay Equity Commission, said in a press release that accompanied the report. "This stark reality isn't just a number — it's a concerning trend contributing to a notable gender disparity among older Canadians, particularly women."

Obviously, Canada is not the only country that has earning and retirement disparities. According to the U.S. Treasury Department, when it comes to Social Security benefits, defined pensions, 401(k)s, individual retirement plans (IRAs) and other retirement plans, women have lower retirement account ownership, receive lower security benefits and own fewer assets than men. Using self-reported data, the Washington-based Institute for Women's Policy Research found that in 2021, the median retirement income for women over 65 was 32.6 percent lower than for men. What's even more depressing is that estimates vary due to limited availability of data. You can't fix a problem you don't study properly.

Canada's not great at intersectional analysis of its retirement income system either, and the *Understand the Gender Pension Gap in Canada* report admits this. That said, people who are racialized, Indigenous and/or immigrants tend to earn less and have lower retirement incomes than their white counterparts. (This is a generalization, as racialized, Indigenous and immigrant groups are not a monolith, and as always, there are differences within the groups.)

There are several more reasons why women don't have as much money as men: They tend to take time away from work for child-bearing, and they carry the majority of the caregiving responsibilities and still do a lot of the domestic labor in the home, which can reduce the time they have for paid work and/or limit their advancement. Do we need to mention the Covid-19 she-cession that saw mostly women losing their jobs and a slow recovery for them finding work? When you lose your job, you are losing time in the labor market where you could be making money, receiving benefits, contributing to your government pension and taking advantage of employer pension plans or registered plan matching. That leads to more senior women living in poverty. The report said that approximately 200,000 more women than men over the age of 65 were living below Canada's low-income threshold in 2020.

And if you're wondering what the low income cut-off is, it was $14,431 in 2020 for a single person in a rural area, and $22,060 for someone living in a city with 500,000 or more people (so, the major and secondary cities). Twenty-one percent of women over 75 had incomes below the low income cut-off, which is 51 percent higher than their male counterparts.

The report also notes that Canada's public pension system was and still is designed for heterosexual couples. It says, and I'm quoting, "the system leverages systemic disadvantage in the labor market, privileges traditional heterosexual marriage and penalizes single mothers." Ahem. In fact, I want to quote a whole paragraph from this report because it lays out that the pension plan was built based on heteronormative coupledom.

> Canada's public pension system was initially designed to meet the retirement income of women through a family model based unambiguously on heterosexual married couples in which a male breadwinner provided support for a full-time homemaker. This model discriminated against women by making their benefits dependent on their male spouse's success in the labor market. But it also explicitly privileged women in heterosexual marriages over those who did not fit that mold, excluding single women, divorced women, many

women in common law relationships and women with same-sex partners.

As expected, this was challenged in the courts, and eventually the pension plan was adapted to include non-heterosexual couples and common-law relationships. Still, there's not a lot there for single people unless they are caregivers. Remember, Betty and her sister can't claim each other's benefits even though they run a shared household.

This isn't to slam federal programs (too much) as they do progress slowly with society, even if they must be taken to court to do so, but as this and the tax code reveals, the couple is the unit around which these programs were built — and it's time for them to catch up with the times.

## SETTING RETIREMENT GOALS

So back to the question of how much you need for retirement when you're single. I went searching for an answer. I met Elke Rubach, a certified financial planner, lawyer and founder of Rubach Wealth, for coffee on a very sweaty July morning.

After we sat down with our coffees and, in my case, a croissant, I said, "Listen, is there a definite number or percentage to figure out how much to save for retirement when you're single? Because every time I ask this question, the answer is 'It depends.'"

She took a sip of her coffee and said, "It does depend." Which is never the answer someone wants to hear when planning their retirement. Ideally, I would love a firm number, but this is real life. "You need to sit down, look at what you want for your retirement and make a plan," she said. "How do you want to live and age? Plus, stop looking at your neighbors." Unless they tell you everything about their finances, you don't know what's going on with them. "They could have gotten two million dollars from their parents," she explained. "And you didn't. You can't plan around what your neighbors do."

When planning for your retirement, Rubach explained that it's important to know how you want to live in retirement. Consider:

- **Age of retirement:** Decide the age you aim to retire. Do you want to retire in the next five years? At 71? Never?
- **Lifestyle:** Determine the lifestyle you want in retirement. Think about travel, hobbies, downsizing, aging in place, etc.
- **Location:** Decide where you want to live. Do you want to stay in your home and in your current city/town/village? Do you want to be a snowbird? Buy a €1 home in Italy and become a renovation YouTuber? Move in with a friend? Pool your resources and become a Golden Girl?

Once you have a sense of the kind of life you'd like to lead, you need to estimate future expenses. I know right now it can be hard to guess the price of eggs next week, let alone at retirement age, but there are tools to help you. Some banks and investing sites offer calculators that can crunch the numbers for you and provide a rough estimate. Wealthsimple has a free one for Canadians, and Vanguard offers one in the U.S.

If you'd like a little more detail and no institutional affiliation, Canadians can use the PERC (personal enhanced retirement calculator) developed by Fred Vettese, actuary and author of several books including *Retirement Income for Life*. After you enter information about your registered and unregistered retirement accounts, it provides two scenarios. The free version gives you an idea of how much income you can draw from all sources. It also assumes your spending does not quite keep pace with inflation in your later years.

The paid version gives you a tailored plan and, according to the website, often produces higher income for you in retirement.

Whether you're using a calculator or estimating things yourself, you'll need an idea of what you might spend. There are also present and future value calculators that can predict how much an amount of money will be worth in the future, or vice versa. That can provide an answer, but the simpler route for all of us, myself included, is to work with a planner and adviser if you can. But here are some future costs to estimate:

- **Basic living expenses:** Will you still have a mortgage and a car, for example? Will your kids be living with you? Will you sell your place and pool your resources with your kids or with friends and buy or rent something? If you live in a condo, do you know the yearly percentage increase for your maintenance fees and if there'll be a special assessment to repair the pool? You should receive annual documents that include the budget and an estimation of any fee increases for the next several years. You'll also need to factor in food and utilities.
- **Healthcare:** As an adviser once told me, you should consider healthcare as a rising cost as you get older and budget accordingly. Expect higher healthcare costs, which may include additional insurance.
- **Leisure and travel:** Budget for hobbies, travel and other activities. Realistically, you're probably not going to change your leisure habits drastically. If you travel now, you'll continue traveling. If you're a crafter, you'll continue crafting.

Next, you'll need to know how much money you have coming in. You'll want to add up:

- **Government pensions:** In Canada, that's CPP and OAS. You can create a My Service Canada account to view and/or print a copy of your CPP Statement of Contributions whenever you want. You can also see how much you would get at 60, 65 and 71 years old based on your current contributions. (In Quebec, you'll have to contact Retraite Québec.) In the U.S., you can estimate how much you'll have coming in from Social Security by going to the Social Security website and playing with the calculator there. It'll ask you questions about your age, current yearly earnings and your future retirement date option. What's cool or terrifying, depending on your situation, is that the Social Security website gives you a choice to see your benefit estimate in today's dollars or inflated dollars.
- **Private pensions:** Include any pension plans you have, no matter how small. I have a locked-in retirement account (LIRA) from a parental-leave contract I did ages ago. I also have a pension from a part-time gig, which doesn't have a lot in it, but if I retire, I will get a little money, which might be enough to cover my monthly electricity bill. If you have a pension plan, you can check with your employer's platform for a projection at ages 60, 65 and 71.
- **Investments:** Figure out your projected income from retirement accounts such as your RRSP, TFSA, 401(k) or IRA. Many investing platforms have calculators that estimate your projected earnings. You can see how much you're likely to earn and even how long your retirement savings will last, if you want to know that. My neighbor once joked to me that her adviser said she had enough funds to live to 92. After that, who knows? Okay, we make some dark jokes.

- **Other sources:** Consider rental income, part-time work and inheritances. But, and this is very big, I'd only factor an inheritance into your financial planning if you've already received it. You might get a future inheritance, but then again, you might not due to debts, bad investments or high medical costs for your parents or grandparents, or they might just spend it. It's their money, not yours.

When you see your projected expenses next to your income and retirement projections, you may want to change your savings rate. Calculators are useful, not reassuring.

Still looking for a rule of thumb for how much to save, I asked Samantha Sykes, a senior investment adviser and financial planner with Raymond James. Sykes said that while a benchmark isn't a replacement for comprehensive planning, it's a quick way to gauge if you're in the ballpark or, as she put it, the parking lot. What Sykes likes to do is look at how much should be saved by X age, based on what income someone is making now, and what they plan on spending at X age, given inflation and spending habits. One example she provided was by age 30, you should have 0.5 to 1 times your salary saved for retirement. At age 35, 1 to 1.5 times your salary saved. Age 40, 1.5 to 2 times your salary saved. Now, if you really want a number, Sykes said some people say that in retirement, you'll need 70 to 80 percent of your pre-retirement income if you're renting and 60 percent if you own your home outright.

You don't have to ask me, what if you can't save that much when you're single and you've already cut expenses down to the barest minimum? What if you did everything right and are still facing a gap between your retirement savings and actual retirement costs?

In Canada, you could theoretically live on CPP and OAS, but it would require constant budgeting. If you think no one can do that, you're wrong. A few years ago, I interviewed my friend Betty McCabe for an article. She has a job that paid her in the low fifties, she has no debt, she works hard, she's been working since she was 16 — so more than 40 years — and she budgets. Yet she has no RRSPs or TFSAs. She's not getting an employer pension. On paper, she has done everything right. Every time she has some money to put away, she gets hit with a crisis, usually medical expenses related to her hearing. McCabe describes herself as hearing impaired and has to upgrade her hearing aids every few years. They can cost between $1,000 to $4,000 per device.

She rents but is looking to buy a condo in her city. The problem is, as it is for many of us, affordability. "The math is a problem," she told me. "And I don't know what that's going to look like until I get closer to having a down payment. And then seeing what the interest rates are and seeing what the housing costs are because they have been going down since the pandemic in my city. It got to a point where units were grossly overvalued and being overpriced by $100,000, and they weren't worth it."

Her plan is to buy a lower-cost condo that has low maintenance fees. If she can pay it off before she retires at 70, then her cost of living would be lower than renting, as she pays up to $1,200 a month. If the condo plan doesn't pan out, she has multiple alternate plans for her retirement. Plan H is looking at retirement homes in her community within her budget. She described plan H as a subsistent, lower-order retirement. "Where, you know, the majority of your money goes to them, but at least they feed you, so you're housed and fed and then you have a couple hundred bucks left, then that's what it is."

She's expecting to live on just CPP and OAS during her retirement. She has some experience from seeing her parents, who are in their eighties, living on just CPP and OAS. She told me her parents' home and cars are paid off, and they live within their means. "So, it's just managing the utilities and taxes," she said. Her parents don't go on vacations and don't go out. McCabe and her brother do convince them to go out for dinner at Swiss Chalet every now and again.

During our conversation, McCabe pointed out that she has a lot of privilege in that she was able to work and pay for things. Still, it's not easy. "I'm technically, based on my annual salary, not part of the working poor, but based on my personal situations and medical situations, that is essentially where [I'm] at, right? And so I always think every advice I've ever seen does not take into account working poor."

She's not wrong, and she's a great example of the fact that personal finance can take us only so far. This is why advocacy for affordable housing is essential, as well as better support for people with disabilities. McCabe's hearing aids should be covered by universal healthcare.

## PLANNING FOR LONG-TERM CARE

A lot of my single friends and I talk about what we're going to do when we get older. We obviously don't want to be a burden on our family and friends, and we are looking at ways to maintain community, manage costs (because Toronto) and have someone nearby just in case. Think Golden Girls, Senior Women Living Together or Japan's Koko Seven, seven women who live close together.

As we saw in the housing chapter, there are many options out there, but we didn't talk about long-term care (LTC) or nursing homes, which are generally thought of as the last stop before, well, death, to be blunt. It's the place you go when you need help with pretty much everything.

The average rent for a standard space in an LTC across Canada was $3,075 a month, according to a 2021 CMHC senior housing survey. That doesn't include a high level of care, which the CMHC defined as 1.5 hours or more a day. Now that was the average cost. In Ontario, all LTC residents must contribute to the cost of the LTC with a co-payment fee based on whether you're in a basic, semi-private or private room. The Ministry of Long-Term Care sets maximum co-payment fees each year, and they are standard for profit and not-for-profit homes across the province.

These fees don't include things like your phone, internet, hairdressing and transportation. So, I guess we'd have to pay to go see our hairdresser or pay for them to come visit us. If you're considered low-income in Ontario and can't afford the co-payment fees, you can apply for financial help.

In the U.S., the median monthly cost for an assisted living facility in 2023 was US$5,350. A nursing home was $8,669 for a semi-private room and $9,733 for a private room. If you want a home healthcare aide, you're looking at $6,292 a month. The median hourly cost of that aide is $33.

Looking at those eye-watering numbers, some people turn to long-term care insurance, which can cover part of your housing costs and the cost of care in your own home and in an LTC. Some policies may also cover rehabilitation and occupational therapy costs. But actuary Fred Vettese says long-term care insurance makes no sense. "It's the opposite of what you want from insurance," he said. "What you want from insurance is to be able to pay a modest amount of premiums, and if something was to happen, the payoff would be huge." But with long-term care insurance, the premiums are very high, and the payoff could be pretty small. When he ran the numbers, he found that it made more sense to put the money you'd be spending on the insurance premiums, which could range from $100 to $250 a month depending on your age and the policy amount, into a savings product like a high-interest savings account or, if you don't need the funds immediately, a guaranteed investment certificate (GIC). Plus, he explained that if you took out a policy in your fifties, then decided you need the money in your sixties or seventies, when you might be paying several hundred dollars a month, or you can't afford the premiums, you get nothing back. All that money you paid is gone. "Nobody wants to take out insurance with the hope of something happening, but if it does, you're happy to have it," he said. "But with long-term care insurance, you're not even happy to have it, and you're still better off if you didn't take it."

Samantha Sykes provided some ideas on how to keep costs lower later in life.

If you're divorced, be aware of any commitments you've made on your retirement accounts based on your prior marital agreements. You may have to pay child support until your youngest child reaches the age of majority, or you may have to give some of your pension to your ex-spouse. Your RRIF, for example, may be considered part of the marital property depending on where you live in Canada. In the U.S., the same rule generally applies. Whether your retirement accounts are up for grabs by your ex-spouse depends on which state you live in, according to the IRS. Whether divorced or not, stay on top of your will, POAs and estate planning to make sure those documents lay out exactly how and where you want to age. This means knowing if you want to and can afford in-home help or if you want to go to an assisted living facility (and which one).

## NOT ALL DOOM AND GLOOM

David Aston, a finance journalist and author of *The Sleep-Easy Retirement Guide*, offered some welcome reassurance that all single people aren't on the Cat Food Express.

Aston said that people, including singles, tend to overestimate how much they'll spend in retirement. That's because most people estimate spending based on their peak income-earning years, usually between age 45 and 54, and many of the expenditures tend to go away around the time you retire. "People tend to have these huge mortgage payments that are a big part of their spending during the peak earning years, and then, for the most part, people are able to pay off the mortgage around the time they retire," he said.

He went on to explain that people tend to forget about work-related costs like commuting, transportation and clothing. Which makes sense — I helped my mother go through her work wardrobe after she retired to see what to keep and repurpose and what to donate. "Also," he said, "you no longer pay employment insurance, and you no longer have to save for retirement because you're already retired. When you have a need for less income in retirement, you also tend to pay less income tax. So, with all of this combined, in general you usually expect your spending [during] retirement to be significantly less than your peak earnings."

Fred Vettese said that household studies have shown that spending lessens as we get older. "Traveling does slow down," he said. "You just do less of it by the time you're 75 because you might be less adventurous. That's true for both singles and couples."

I asked Vettese if there were any spending patterns that differed between couples and single people in retirement. "The amount that you're spending, it's not going to be half as much," he said. "All the academic studies tend to suggest that the spending by a household is proportional to the square root of the number of people in the household. So, if you got two people in the household, you're going to be spending 1.4 times as much as for one person. That means that if going down from two people to one person, you're going to be spending about 30 percent less."

It's not all grumbling and complaining that couples have it better than single people, even though I spent the first part of this chapter doing just that. Yes, couples, especially retired ones, do have some advantages with income splitting and spousal retirement plan contributions, but that only happens in retirement.

Singles have an advantage if they don't have kids. Aston said they may have a fair bit of disposable income relative to couples who have kids. That's because kids are expensive. You want a home with a backyard for them to run around in, if you can afford it, and there are all the activities you sign them up for. They become teenagers and inhale the fridge. They grow all the time until they're 18, if you're lucky. I remember when my eldest nibling needed emergency winter boots because theirs were too small. The fact that they had the same size foot as me made me glare at them suspiciously, which they found amusing. In 2023, Statistics Canada found the average cost of raising a child to age 17 was $293,000 in a two-parent, two-child family. For a solo parent, the average was $231,260 if the parent earned under $83,000 annually, and $372,110 if they earned over $83,000.

"For single people who don't have kids, there can be the opportunity to save more in their peak earning years relative to couples of similar ages who have kids," Aston said. It's an opportunity to save money sooner and let the magic of compound interest or time in the stock market make that money grow.

While we were talking, I admitted it's easier to be positive about saving for retirement with younger single people, as they have more time to invest and spend time in the market. But then I read reports that senior women have a higher risk of sliding into poverty even if they've done everything right. Aston said that it's about maintaining the right balance between hopefulness and reality: "The path isn't necessarily easy, but I think for most people, there's a way—especially for people that have the advantages of education and professional career opportunities." He explained that for most people, there is a reasonable path to retirement, but they'll likely have to make some hard choices along the way. It becomes a balance of what people want to do and what they need to do to make income. Someone who has some knowledge about finances could have a big advantage over someone without that knowledge.

Vettese also pointed out, "Single people maybe don't have as much of a reason to worry about trying to save money for the next generation. Couples may have to take care of a loved one and may also want to pass on some money." That might mean couples with dependents might be focused on ensuring there's money left as a legacy for the next generation. Single people sans children can save and spend it all, if they want.

## THE TAKEAWAYS

- Don't fear the calculators! Go play with them and figure out your retirement plan.
- The same goes for investing. Figure out what kind of investor you are and get to it. The sooner you start, the more time you have for your money to multiply.
- Try to understand what you'd like your retirement to look like. Not your neighbor's retirement, yours. One of my neighbors wants to move out of the city. I don't. There's no comparison.
- Policies get changed when people speak up about them: Keep fighting for affordable housing, pay equity and comprehensive healthcare that will ensure people don't have to work until the grave.

## CHAPTER 9

# Leaving a Legacy

I asked my single friends, "Do you think of leaving a legacy, and if so, what would that look like?" And I accidentally increased my friends' therapy bills and ratcheted up the angst. Kristin straight-up told me, "Every one of your prompts sends me into an existential crisis," followed by a loud "SAAAME" from Robin. (Sorry, you two). My sister-in-law responded, "Why is one needed? A rhetorical question. I always say time on this rock is limited and the expiry date is unknown." Caitlin said that's what her kids are for, while my brother said, "To crush my enemies, see them driven before me and to hear the lamentations of their women." (Can you tell he's my younger brother?)

As much as I love drama (provided it's not mine), I didn't mean to cause a crisis among my single friends. But it is something I think about. It's easy to leave a legacy when you have kids, providing they outlive you, or when you're very involved with other kiddos in your circle. Of course, you could argue that your digital footprint is your legacy as it does show what you valued and what you were thinking about. Unless there's a massive electromagnetic pulse that destroys everything or AI deletes us all. Hmm.

There was a meme on TikTok and Reddit saying that people only remember you for three generations, which is not true for everyone. One Medium article asked its readers, "Do you know the life and the name of your great-grandfather?" Yes, I do. It's Henry Sylvester Williams, and my great-grandmother's name was Agnes Powell. It helps that Henry did some spectacular things when he was alive like organize the first pan-African conference and the Coloured Hockey League and has a green plaque in London as he was one of the first Black politicians there. Most of us aren't doing that. Yes, at some point most of us will be forgotten and that's totally fine, but that doesn't mean we don't want to be remembered positively, at least for a while.

The idea of leaving a legacy is a bit like doing your will. It can make you confront your mortality, which a lot of people aren't willing to do. In talking to various advisers, certain things about legacy came up. Women were more open to having the legacy conversation than men. The one thing is that women often wonder if they have enough money to create that legacy. But not all legacies require wealth.

I teach part-time, so twice a year I have up to 20 students in my class for 14 weeks. I really enjoy teaching — grading, not so much. I'm not going to say that I have some massive impact on my students, but I like to think that I play a small, useful role as they move on to their careers.

Teaching reminds me of Sister Phyllis Wharfe, the principal of my secondary school and a nun with the Sisters of St. Joseph of Cluny. Yes, I'm a convent girl (IYKYK). Sister Phyllis had a doctorate, and when she wasn't teaching, she was low-key being terrifying. She was the only person who could say "Miss Sylvestre-Williams" ominously. Actually, she said all our last names ominously. One day after I had already graduated, I was visiting the school to pick up my sister. I went to the office to sign in, and Sister Phyllis was there. We had a lovely chat, and I told her I was starting university later that year. She had written me a really nice recommendation letter, so I think she was pleased that I had gotten in. I remember asking her if she scared deliberately. "Of course," she said, extremely pleasantly, smiling the whole time. It was jarring, because in my seven years in secondary school, her smiles were few and far between.

I wasn't surprised. This was the woman who once scolded my class year because instead of studying for our A-levels, we would play cards, betting with matches or pennies. She had a goal for us to move on to postsecondary education or work. We were going to university or college if we could afford it, or we were going to get a good job. She and Mom were on the same wavelength.

Sister Phyllis died in 2019, and she left a powerful legacy as an educator. Her students are all around the world, being doctors, lawyers, accountants, educators, C-suite execs, running their own businesses, being parents and aunts. In a way, you could say she also had an influence on our finances as well. She taught us to speak our minds and not be afraid to be smart or ask for what we want. I'm not sure she succeeded with me when it came to religion, but overall, hers is a great legacy and I'm proud to have been one of her students.

Financial planner Elke Rubach once told me that legacy starts with understanding your or your family's values. While most of us have an idea of what our values are by how we behave, it can be hard to articulate them. One idea I really like is rich aunties. It's a term that is believed to have originated with Rachel Cargle, who in 2020 created Rich Auntie Supreme, a website and social media presence that bills itself as "a space to celebrate and be in community with those women who choose a journey of being child-free and indulgence in the villages around them."

When I spoke to financial planner Jackie Porter for an article on rich aunties, she said that studies have shown that these women tend to have a higher net worth, more homeownership and investments. (The article was specifically about aunties, but it applies to single uncles.) She went on to say that not having children and being financially driven affords rich aunties the time and the funds to invest in themselves and their communities. When Porter and I reconnected, we chatted more about legacy, both financial and intangible. Porter points out that part of leaving a legacy is planning well. That means having your money do the work for you, giving yourself more time so you can enjoy the life you want and then building the legacy you want.

One of the reasons why people tend to think of legacies in financial terms is because that's what has been promoted. Think about all the news reports of people leaving millions or billions of dollars to their favorite charity, or leaving their art collection or their papers to a museum. Porter said your legacy could be passing on family heirlooms and helping the recipients understand why and what they meant to you. Whatever you choose to do, it's about building a memory, and hopefully that memory inspires the people that you leave behind.

"I think it starts with being active in community, figuring out how you can champion something that you passionately care about, so that someone can take the baton and continue on," she said. It could be volunteering for a favorite charity, doing the annual cleanup of your community or writing, as she described it, "a big check." Porter explained, "So for me, it's writing big checks to charity and having that be a memory that hopefully I can inspire in my nieces and young people that I deal with." Another way of leaving a legacy is to mentor. "It's so important. You have so much to offer, so offer it to people who are behind you, who don't necessarily have guidance. Even if they have parents, they might not have guidance."

She also blew my mind when she pointed out that leaving a mess for someone to clean up is a type of legacy. "I'm actually quite conscious, because I don't have children, that I don't want too much stuff," she said. You may have heard of döstädning, known in English as Swedish death cleaning, the KonMari Method's goth cousin, which empowers us to streamline our possessions so our loved ones don't have to. Looking around my apartment, I have an excessive amount of magazines, books and plants. I definitely have stuff. Mom once called me a collector.

Porter went on to say, "I live in a triplex, and I want to force myself to not accumulate too much stuff, because someone else is going to freaking have to deal with it. Somebody asked me the other day if I was going to buy a house in Antigua because I'd visited there two times in the last year. I asked them if they were kidding. Who's gonna deal with my estate? I don't want someone flying to try and figure out the different tax laws." Understandable as, if that was the case, it would take forever as even the law moves at Caribbean time.

Porter also suggested writing a last letter, a final list of instructions that make it clear what you want. You can tell people where to find your things, who gets your jewelry and even instructions like sending birthday cards to friends and family after your death. You can also list your death wishes in the letter. "For example, I want to be cremated," she said. "I do not want to be that dead person that people said, 'You know, Jackie, she looked pretty good.' Nobody looks pretty good dead, as far as I'm concerned." She has a plan. "Put a picture of me looking fly and have people remember that, because I get it. People want to see a body, but that's not how I want to be seen. So it's about me."

Reader, I'm not going to lie, I laughed pretty hard at that because, yeah, you look dead. Why not have all your hottest selfies and pictures of you laughing with friends blown up? Have a party.

So, clean your place out before you go, write that letter, put some money aside to have a party and get some amazing pictures done so people can remember you at your flyest.

## INTANGIBLE INHERITANCES

I'm at the age of going to funerals for my friends' parents. At the time of writing this, my parents are here, but I live in low-key fear of the day I lose them. I will never be ready. I've started recording some of our conversations — just the random stuff we talk about, our days, what they're doing, what I'm doing, Mom occasionally asking me to buy something off Amazon, Dad and I talking about regrouting the bathtub or maybe just going for Bath Fitters, the shelf he's cutting down and staining so I can use it under my television, and them asking me how many doubles I want when we visit each other next. (The answer is always yes to doubles, medium pepper, then a discussion about the number.)

I just want their voices around for decades to come, and I think it would be nice to have the recordings to pass over to my brother and sister-in-law and the kids if they want them. Maybe their kids if they have them. Yes, it's weird and creepy; no, I'm not sorry. I think about this a lot because my sister died nearly 30 years ago, and we have pictures, letters and her things, but I don't remember what her voice sounded like. I would have liked to hear her voice in the last few years.

Elena Iacono launched her company, LegacyNex, in 2024, to help clients define and document their nonfinancial legacy — "your stories, wisdom and experiences," as it says on her website. "By documenting your most meaningful messages, you offer those dearest to you a lasting gift that provides guidance, inspiration, comfort and connection."

Even if you're worried about future cash flow, LegacyNex argues you have things to offer those you leave behind. "We all have something to share, and we all have a legacy to convey," Iacono said.

She challenges people to think about what's the biggest lesson or the biggest enlightenment that they've had in their lives and how they should share it: "We know that people today are struggling to find role models that they can really trust and turn to and learn from. The biggest driver of personal growth is learning from each other." She wants to encourage people of all demographics to think about what small impact they can have, and how they can share to inspire better habits or behaviors in others. "I think that's the essence of legacy. It's not about finances or money. Yes, it could be high-net-worth people that have a lot to leave financially, but I think we all have something to share from a story perspective."

When Iacono is working with someone, after the initial consultation, her client gets a planning document. "It's the planning piece that gets them thinking in three sections," she said. "What impact do you want to have or make? What exactly do you want to share?" Part of it, she told me, was offering structure and some prompts. "I think it's really important to step back and ask, 'What do you want people to do with this information?' And, most importantly, 'What type of feelings or change in behaviors do you want to elicit?'"

She has really thought about the end user who's going to get the information. "Questions the beneficiary should ask are 'What do you want me to do with this stuff?' 'How do I live up to it in a way that makes sense for me?' And most importantly, 'How do I continue to reflect on all these good learnings once the person is gone and I don't forget the essence of who this person was?'"

In fact, Iacono recommended having the beneficiary involved in the process. The customer can bring their beneficiary to this discussion, and they can interview each other. The end document will be given to the client or to the beneficiary, and they can either distribute it to people in advance or they can have it tucked away with their will.

I asked Iacono what a single person might include if they have no descendants. "I would say people can document their personal stories, their perspectives, whatever they want to share with community organizations that matter to them," she said. "They could leave it to either universities or undergraduate schools that they went to, paying it forward to future students, to really offer skills, leadership, insights, whatever it is to inspire greatness in the next generation. So, I think that people can absolutely share their perspectives."

## THE SMALL STUFF THAT ISN'T SMALL AT ALL

I didn't go to primary or secondary school in Canada, so I was surprised when the kids in my life had to do a family tree. It was fun sitting with my eldest nibling and tracing our family back five generations. I appreciated the quality time spent and sharing our ancestors with them. It led to several conversations confirming the names of my great-grandparents with my parents, who were also there helping out. As a result, I've become the de facto holder of the family lore. When I visit my parents, they tell me stories about their parents, grandparents, great-uncles, great-aunts and all the cousins, of whom there are a lot. It's something I've come to appreciate, and I've already started passing these stories down to my niblings, who don't really care at the moment, but they humor me in between playing Minecraft, War Machines and Roblox.

Just putting in the time and being a positive presence in people's lives can be a legacy. If you're not a people person but love animals, why not let your legacy be fostering animals? One of my friends fosters dogs, and you can see the difference between when the dogs arrive and when they go to their forever home. Even if you don't have a lot of money to leave a financial legacy, you can still have a positive impact on your immediate and extended circles of two- and four-legged beings.

One friend said that she cares about what she does now while she's alive: "I try to do no harm. And if I can, make things better even if it's in a small way. I've always found it confusing that people care about what happens after they are gone. I'm not criticizing if people care about legacy; it's just not in my thoughts. Maybe I've been living too long in the lower end of Maslow's hierarchy of needs to have gotten to that point. If by legacy you mean money, then again, if I had extra to spare, I'd be using it to make things better for others now."

Another friend, Jo, said their legacy isn't going to be money. It's going to be the people in their life: "Something that changed my life (shockingly) was one week in the 7 Habits of Highly Effective People course, where I had to craft a mission statement. The exercise, I believe, was 'begin with the end in mind,' and you had to envision what people were saying about you at your funeral (presuming you'd lived your best life). Mine kept coming back to a few key words: bold, authentic, fearless and writing. So, my mission statement became 'To inspire people to live bold and authentic lives through my fearless example and writing.' I crafted that 20 years ago, and it's still as true today as it was then, even more so. That will be my legacy. I have had kids come up to me in high schools after my gender talks and hug me and tell me I changed their lives. It's mind-blowing. So yeah, if I die today, I die happy and fulfilled."

There are a few reasons I wanted to finish by talking about legacy in a book about finances. Money does underpin a lot of what we do and the decisions that we make, because unfortunately we live in a capitalist society. But ultimately money is just a tool that we use, not an end in itself. If you die without much money left in your coffers, that's okay. (Some would even call that acing the assignment because you cannot take it with you. And if you try, be prepared to be visited by graverobbers or to have your body and your stuff displayed in a museum centuries from now. Creepy.) A lot of financial decisions are driven by nonfinancial values. Thinking about your legacy can inform your spending decisions and your financial and retirement planning.

Lastly, in a world that often treats single people as marginal or unworthy and makes it harder for us to eke out a living, know that when it comes to relationships and experiences, your life can still be impossibly rich.

# Acknowledgments

I learned that the actual sitting down and the writing of a book is a solo (ha) process but everything else that makes a book come to life is thanks to having a community of people around you.

My parents, Wayne and Gayle Sylvestre-Williams, especially my mother, who told me for years to write a book.

The board of directors consisting of Robin, Robin (yes, there are two), Kate, Celia, Diane, Amanda and Aliza, especially Aliza, who introduced me to Kelvin. Everyone else for their suggestions, comments and eyeballs on several paragraphs that are now in this book.

Kelvin Kong, my agent who thought the world needed this book, held my hand through the proposal process and listens to me when I stream-of-consciousness at him on WhatsApp.

Amy Fallon, we connected on LinkedIn as fellow journalists, and when I put out a call for help with the book, she hooked me up with information and people to talk with.

Helen Duffy for their contacts and connections for this book.

Samantha Sykes, Jackie Porter and Elke Rubach for talking to me about retirement planning and for generally being amazing advisers.

Jen Knoch for being an amazing editor.

Nicholas Sylvestre-Williams and Barbara Sylvestre-Williams for many things: being my family, supporting me and respecting my time as a single person.

To the kids. I love you dearly.

Anne Cayer, Ryan Thomas, Tiffany, Alex and Jon for being cheerleaders from day one.

Gail McInnes for being my sounding board, offering advice and being an overall amazing person.

Nathalie Atkinson, who sends me links on being single, is an amazing resource on all things and is an amazing person. Thank you, Nathalie, especially for connecting me with Melissa.

Melissa Leong who took the time to speak with me about the book process including the why of doing a book. She played a large role in my publishing decisions.

All my readers of *The Budgette.* You have kept me going for the last six years, which led to this book you hold right now.

David Aston not only for talking with me for the book but for also taking the time to chat with me about the book-writing process.

Fred Vettese for walking me through retirement planning.

Susy Fossati, etiquette expert.

Martha Casson for sharing her story.

Pat Dunn for talking to me about Senior Women Living Together.

Lisa Hannam and the MoneySense team for their support. They commissioned an article about solo spending when many media outlets weren't thinking about us. That story inspired a huge Reddit thread, which was wild.

Elena Iocco, for being an amazing cheerleader. Thank you, Elena, for reading the newsletter and just being you.

Betty, Jo, Caitlin, Aya, Kirsten and all the others for sharing their thoughts and answers when I put out the call. Thank you.

# References

## INTRODUCTION

American Psychological Association. "APA Survey Shows Money Stress Weighing on Americans' Health Nationwide." February 4, 2015. https://www.apa.org/news/press/releases/2015/02/money-stress.

Cain, Sian. "Women Are Happier without Children or a Spouse, Says Happiness Expert." *The Guardian*, May 25, 2019. https://www.theguardian.com/lifeandstyle/2019/may/25/women-happier-without-children-or-a-spouse-happiness-expert.

Dalhousie University et al. *Canada's Food Price Report*, 12th edition. 2022. https://cdn.dal.ca/content/dam/dalhousie/pdf/sites/agri-food/Food%20Price%20Report%20-%20EN%202022.pdf.

FP Canada. "FP Canada™ 2025 Financial Stress Index Reveals Top Financial Stressors, Barriers and Generational Differences." March 18, 2025. https://www.fpcanada.ca/newsdetail/fp-canada--2025-financial-stress-index-reveals-top-financial-stressors--barriers-and-generational-differences.

Mental Health Foundation. "Financial Strain Is Driving the UK's Anxiety." May 15, 2023. https://www.mentalhealth .org.uk/about-us/news/financial-strain-driving-uks-anxiety.

National Labor Relations Board. "Your Rights to Discuss Wages." Accessed May 7, 2025. https://www.nlrb.gov/about -nlrb/rights-we-protect/your-rights/your-rights-to-discuss -wages.

Rentals.ca. "May 2025 Rentals.ca Rent Report." Accessed May 20, 2025. https://rentals.ca/national-rent-report.

Statistics Canada. "Income Statistics by Selected Family Type, 2018 and 2019." Accessed May 20, 2025. https://www150 .statcan.gc.ca/n1/daily-quotidien/210323/t001a-eng.htm.

Statistics Canada. "Living Solo." StatsCAN Plus, September 29, 2022.

*Toronto Star.* "Canada Has More Solo Agers Than Almost Any Other Country. Here's What It's Like Growing Old Alone." April 10, 2025. https://www.thestar.com/news/canada /watch-canada-has-more-solo-agers-than-almost-any-other -country-here-s-what-it/article_d320cd5a-540e-4fa9-a2f9 -2d71c2bec605.html.

Wells Fargo. "The Wells Fargo Money Study." September 5– October 3, 2023. https://sites.wf.com/wfmoneystudy/.

Xinhua. "Record Number of Japanese Are Living Alone: Survey." July 5, 2024. https://english.news.cn/20240705/dca0ee8c7ada 42e1880b4f81dd74943c/c.html.

## CHAPTER 2

Adkins, Frankie. "How to Make Multigenerational Living a Success." BBC Future, May 25, 2023. https://www.bbc.com /future/article/20230525-how-to-make-multigenerational -living-a-success.

Baig, Khulud, et al. *An Intersectional Feminist Housing Agenda for Canada: A Briefing Guide for Canada's Housing Minister.* Women's National Housing & Homelessness Network, 2021. https://womenshomelessness.ca/wp-content/uploads/An-Intersectional-Feminist-Housing-Agenda.pdf.

Canadian Press. "Canadian Home Value Has Doubled Since 2000: Report." *The Globe and Mail*, November 7, 2011. https://www.theglobeandmail.com/real-estate/the-market/canadian-home-value-has-doubled-since-2000-report/article4249097/.

Carney, Scott. "The Nuclear Family Was a Mistake." *The Atlantic*, March 2020. https://www.theatlantic.com/magazine/archive/2020/03/the-nuclear-family-was-a-mistake/605536/.

Case, Cheryll. "A Woman's Right to Housing." In *House Divided: How the Missing Middle Will Solve Toronto's Affordability Crisis*, edited by Alex Bozikovic, Cheryll Case, John Lorinc and Annabel Vaughan. Coach House, 2019.

Cooper, Sean. "How Much You Need to Earn to Afford a Home in Toronto and the GTA." MoneySense, March 20, 2024. https://www.moneysense.ca/spend/real-estate/how-much-you-need-to-afford-a-home-in-toronto/.

Davis, Michelle R., AARP. "Despite Pandemic, Percentage of Older Adults Who Want to Age in Place." November 18, 2021. https://www.aarp.org/home-family/your-home/info-2021/home-and-community-preferences-survey.html.

Eliasson, Sara. "Gender Perspectives Often Ignored in Urban Planning." Mistra Urban Futures, September 1, 2017. https://www.mistraurbanfutures.org/en/content/gender-perspectives-often-ignored-urban-planning.

Grim, Quinlan. "The Average Home Mortgage Payment in 2024: US vs. Canada." GoBanking Rates, August 31, 2024.

https://finance.yahoo.com/news/average-home-mortgage
-payment-2024-160040997.html.

Guzman, Gloria, and Melissa Kollar. "Income in the United States: 2023. Current Population Reports, P60-282." U.S. Census Bureau, September 2024. https://www.census.gov/library /publications/2024/demo/p60-282.html.

Housing International. "United States of America." Housing International. Accessed May 7, 2025. https://www.housing international.coop/co-ops/united-states-of-america/.

International Cooperative Alliance. "Facts and Figures." Accessed May 7, 2025. https://ica.coop/en/cooperatives/facts-and -figures.

Kassam, Ashifa. "'Lens of a singleton': Belgian Council to Focus on Those Who Live Alone." *The Guardian*, February 14, 2024. https://www.theguardian.com/world/2024/feb/14/lens -singleton-belgian-council-focus-live-alone.

Langille, Kaley. "Here's the Income Bracket You Need to Afford a Home in Major Canadian Cities." Ontario Housing Market, November 24, 2024. https://ontariohousingmarket .com/2024/11/24/heres-the-income-bracket-you-need-to -afford-a-home-in-major-canadian-cities/.

National Low Income Housing Coalition. *The Gap: A Shortage of Affordable Homes*. March 2025. https://nlihc.org/gap.

Peesker, Saira. "Forget Downsizing: Canadian Seniors Staying in Large Houses Well into Their 80s, Due in Part to Lack of Options." *Globe and Mail*, February 11, 2024. https://www .theglobeandmail.com/investing/personal-finance/retirement /article-forget-downsizing-canadian-seniors-staying-in-large -houses-well-into/.

Pew Charitable Trusts. "Survey Finds Large Majorities Favor Policies to Enable More Housing." November 30, 2023.

https://www.pewtrusts.org/en/research-and-analysis/articles/2023/11/30/survey-finds-large-majorities-favor-policies-to-enable-more-housing.

Pew Research Center. "Urban, Suburban and Rural Residents' Views on Key Social and Political Issues." May 22, 2018. https://www.pewresearch.org/social-trends/2018/05/22/urban-suburban-and-rural-residents-views-on-key-social-and-political-issues/.

Scotiabank. "How Much Should I Budget for Home Maintenance Costs?" Accessed May 7, 2025. https://www.scotiabank.com/ca/en/personal/advice-plus/features/posts.how-much-should-i-budget-for-home-maintenance-costs.html.

Scott, Brianna. "Buying a Home Became a Key Way to Build Wealth. What Happens When You Can't?" NPR. January 9, 2023. https://www.npr.org/2023/01/09/1147453685/house-housing-property-prices-to-buy-rent.

Shea, Courtney. "Toronto's Zoning Laws Are About to Change. Here's What That Means for Multiplexes." *Toronto Life*, March 15, 2023. https://torontolife.com/city/zoning-laws-toronto-multiplexes-gregg-lintern/.

Sheppard, Eddie. "67% of Canadians Recognize Homelessness as a Housing Issue Needing Immediate Action." Abacus Data. January 31, 2025. https://abacusdata.ca/canadians-recognize-homelessness-as-a-housing-issue-needing-immediate-action/.

Social Housing Vienna. "History." Socialhousing.wien. Accessed May 7, 2025. https://socialhousing.wien/city-profile/history.

Statista. "Median Annual Family Income in Canada from 1990 to 2022." Accessed May 7, 2025. https://www.statista.com/statistics/465739/median-annual-family-income-in-canada-since-1990/.

Storeys. "Canada Home Price Change 2020–2023." Accessed May 7, 2025. https://storeys.com/canada-home-price-change -2020-2023/.

Van den Bossche, Yelene. *The Political Economy of Single Person Households: How Unadjusted Governmental Policies Affect Singles.* 2015.

## CHAPTER 3

Food Banks Canada. "HungerCount: Overall Findings." Accessed May 7, 2025. https://foodbankscanada.ca/hunger count/overall-findings/.

Royal Bank of Canada. "Where Did My Money Go? The Cost of Being Single in Canada." Accessed May 20, 2025. https://www.rbcroyalbank.com/en-ca/my-money-matters /life-events/finances-and-relationships/marriage/where-did -my-money-go-the-cost-of-being-single-in-canada/.

U.S. Department of Agriculture, Economic Research Service. "Key Statistics & Graphics: Food Security in the U.S." Accessed May 7, 2025. https://www.ers.usda.gov/topics/food-nutrition -assistance/food-security-in-the-us/key-statistics-graphics.

## CHAPTER 4

Connelly, M.P. "Women in the Labour Force." *Canadian Encyclopedia*, February 7, 2006. https://www.thecanadian encyclopedia.ca/en/article/women-in-the-labour-force/.

Government of Canada. "Conjugal Relationships." Accessed May 20, 2025. https://www.canada.ca/en/immigration-refugees -citizenship/corporate/publications-manuals/operational -bulletins-manuals/permanent-residence/non-economic-classes /family-class-determining-spouse/assessing-conjugal.html.

Phipps, Lisa. "Cracking the Conjugal Myths: What Does It Mean for Attribution Rules?" *Canadian Tax Journal* 50, no. 3 (2001): 1031–1039.

## CHAPTER 5

Clark, Max Zahn. "Solo Travel Is on the Rise. Hotels Are Responding." Yahoo Finance, May 9, 2025. https://finance.yahoo.com/news/solo-travel-rise-hotels-responding-00274 1988.html.

Edenedo, Nicole. "Tour Operators Report High Demand for Solo Travel." *Travel Weekly*, May 5, 2023. https://www.travelweekly.com/Travel-News/Tour-Operators/Tour-operators-report-high-demand-for-solo-travel-2147152202.

Hunter, Marnie. "Solo Flyers Often Pay Higher Fares. US Airlines Are Starting to Notice." CNN, May 30, 2025. https://www.cnn.com/2025/05/30/travel/solo-flyers-higher-fares-us-airlines.

Janchill, Johanna. "Solo on the Seas: Ships Roll Out More Amenities and Balconies for Singles." *Travel Weekly*, August 4, 2021. https://www.travelweekly.com/Cruise-Travel/Solo-on-the-seas-Ships-roll-out-more-amenities-and-balconies-for-singles.

Kopun, Francine. "More People in Toronto Are Eating Alone in Restaurants; the Trend Is Expected to Rise." *Toronto Star*, November 15, 2024. https://www.thestar.com/news/gta/more-people-in-toronto-are-eating-alone-in-restaurants-the-trend-is-expected-to-rise/article_1fc0a15e-7c49-11ef-b8a6-23be02477088.html.

Kubiak, Paloma. "Solo Travellers Pay a Near 90% Premium for Their Holidays." YourMoney.com, January 12, 2023. https://www.yourmoney.com/household-bills/solo-travellers-pay-a-nearly-90-premium/.

Nesbitt, Tracey. "Best Accommodation for Solo Travelers." Solo
    Traveler World. Accessed May 7, 2025. https://solotraveler
    world.com/best-accommodation-for-solo-travelers/.
Phocus Wire. "What Billions of GDS Data Signals Tell Us
    About Solo Traveling." Accessed May 20, 2025. https://www
    .phocuswire.com/Travel-booking-behavior-data-signals.
Potter, Kyle. "New Delta Pricing Quirk Charges Solo & Business
    Travelers More." Thrifty Traveler, May 28, 2025. https://
    thriftytraveler.com/news/airlines/delta-pricing-quirk/.
Retail Insider. "Canadian Restaurants Poised to Capitalize
    on Rising Solo Dining Trend." August 12, 2024. https://
    retail-insider.com/bulletin/2024/08/canadian-restaurants
    -poised-to-capitalize-on-rising-solo-dining-trend/.

**CHAPTER 6**

Canadian Cancer Society. "Cost of Cancer." Accessed May 7, 2025.
    https://cancer.ca/en/get-involved/advocacy/cost-of-cancer.
"Los Angeles Fire Insurance Smoke Damage." *Washington Post*,
    February 21, 2025. https://www.washingtonpost.com/weather
    /2025/02/21/los-angeles-fire-insurance-smoke-damage/.

**CHAPTER 7**

Angus Reid Institute. "Lacking the Will: Half of Canadians
    Say They Don't Have a Last Will and Testament, Including
    One-in-Five Aged 55+." March 7, 2023. https://angusreid
    .org/canada-will-testament-intestate-dying-without-will/.
Mair, Chazz. "Secondhand Sorrow: The Gift of Nine Night."
    Order of the Good Death, July 9, 2021. https://www.orderof
    thegooddeath.com/article/secondhand-sorrow-the-gift-of
    -nine-night/.

Parman, Larry. "Survey: Two-Thirds of Americans Don't Have Wills or Trusts." Parman & Easterday, July 7, 2022. https://www.parmanlaw.com/survey-two-thirds-of-americans-dont-have-wills-or-trusts/.


## CHAPTER 8

Canada Life. "What Happens to Your Pension after a Divorce?" Accessed May 7, 2025. https://www.canadalife.com/investing-saving/retirement/pension-plans/what-happens-pension-divorce.html.

CareScout. "Cost of Care." Accessed May 7, 2025. https://www.carescout.com/cost-of-care.

Oishi, Yukako. "Friends Living Nearby Scheme in Japan: Women Maintain Groups to Help Each Other as They Age." Asia News Network, March 4, 2024. https://asianews.network/friends-living-nearby-scheme-in-japan-women-maintain-groups-to-help-each-other-as-they-age/.

Pay Equity Office, Ontario. "Ontario's Pay Equity Office Unveils a Hidden Inequality: 'The Gender Pension Gap.'" May 15, 2024. https://www.newswire.ca/news-releases/ontario-s-pay-equity-office-unveils-a-hidden-inequality-the-gender-pension-gap--852930980.html.

Pay Equity Office, Ontario. *Understanding the Gender Pension Gap in Canada.* May 2024. https://payequity.gov.on.ca/wp-content/uploads/2024/06/PEO_Understanding-the-Gender-Pension-Gap-in-Canada-EN-1.pdf.

U.S. Department of the Treasury. "Spotlighting Women's Retirement Security." Accessed May 7, 2025. https://home.treasury.gov/news/featured-stories/spotlighting-womens-retirement-security.

# Index